JUDSON PRESS

PUBLISHERS SINCE 1824

Leading Your African American Church through
Pastoral
Transition

Ralph C. Watkins

Foreword by Samuel B. McKinney
Afterword by Walter L. Parrish III

JUDSON PRESS
PUBLISHERS SINCE 1824
VALLEY FORGE, PA

LEADING YOUR AFRICAN AMERICAN CHURCH THROUGH PASTORAL TRANSITION

© 2010 by Judson Press, Valley Forge, PA 19482-0851

Judson Press and the author have made every effort to trace the ownership of all quotes. In the event of a question arising from the use of a quote, we regret any error made and will be pleased to make the necessary correction in future printings and editions of this book.

Bible quotations in this volume are from The New Revised Standard Version Bible, copyright 1989, Division of Christian Education of the National Council of Churches of Christ in the United States of America. Used by permission. All rights reserved.

Interior design by Crystal Devine.

Cover design by Tobias Becker and Bird Box Graphic Design. www.birdboxdesign.com.

Library of Congress Cataloging-in-Publication Data

Watkins, Ralph C.
    Leading your African American church through pastoral transition / Ralph C. Watkins ; foreword by Samuel B. McKinney ; afterword by Walter L. Parrish III. -- 1st ed.
        p. cm.
    ISBN 978-0-8170-1641-8 (pbk.: alk. paper) 1. African American churches. 2. Clergy--Appointment, call, and election. I. Title.
    BR563.N4W358 2010
    254--dc22

                        2010014937

Printed in the U.S.A.
First Edition, 2010.

To the love of my life, my wife, Dr. Vanessa Watkins.
Vanessa, you have been with me through every transition.
Thanks for riding with me.

Contents

Foreword

Whether by congregational election, judicatory assignment, or a complex joint process involving the local church and a regional or denominational group, the process of establishing a pastor in a new pulpit can be a dramatic and traumatic moment in the life of a congregation. Pastoral transitions can be smooth, like when Jesus turned water into wine, or they may be as rough as a storm on the sea of Galilee, but every transition has potentially far-reaching consequences for the members of the congregation, the church leadership, the pastoral family, and the greater community. So, conversations need to be introduced, thorough investigations need to be done, and the reality and impact of what a pastoral transition means need to be understood by all involved in the process.

A deep debt of gratitude must be extended to Ralph C. Watkins, a respected pastor, preacher, and scholar in the African Methodist Episcopal communion, for the preparation of this tremendous guide, *Leading Your African American Church through Pastoral Transition*. Rev. Dr. Watkins went to great lengths to analyze pastoral transitions in as many aspects as possible. As a result, he has created a detailed roadmap, a modern-day GPS to guide ministerial change, mobility, and acceptance, with roles to be fulfilled and rules to be followed.

Without question, change is not easy. The old adage says, "Take change by the hand before it takes you by the throat." Translation: transitions are moving forces; they are not stale, static, or stationary. The same could be said for ministry, the pastorate, and preachers that are in the midst of life-changing decisions. Transition is an active process, and it is in motion long before a pastor goes to serve a new congregation. Transition is underway while one is actively involved in a pastorate, and even when one retires. So this book is relevant for all pastors, their families, church leaders, and congregants.

I find this book both informational and compelling, but especially engaging are the five ecumenical testimonies from pastors representing different faith traditions, namely, the apostolic, the Methodist Episcopal, and the free church, including Baptists, United Church of Christ, and Disciples of Christ. The telling stories and graphic testimonies of the five pastors who share the successes and failures they experienced will help to illuminate the paths others will tread—and I believe may ultimately make those travels easier. Because of the importance of its topic, *Leading Your African American Church through Pastoral Transition* should be required reading for all denominational leaders, seminarians, church officers, pastoral review and pulpit search committees, and pastors in any point of their own ministry journey.

Transitioning is never a "cake walk." I am intimately aquatinted with this journey and I have walked its well-worn roads, for I am a pastor who has transitioned in the ministry and in the pastorate. Based on such experiences, I am convinced that reading this book will be more than a blessing to those who take its contents seriously and adhere to its tenets. It certainly blessed me.

Libertas Postea Pax
Rev. Dr. Samuel B. McKinney
Pastor Emeritus
Mount Zion Baptist Church of Seattle

Preface

When I think about going to a new church, I have mixed emotions. I remember the joy I had when Bishop Richard Allen Hilderbrand sent me to my first church back in 1992. I was sent to a closed church—a church whose doors had been shut and locked—and I was delighted to be there. After graduating from seminary, I was ordained an elder in the African Methodist Episcopal (AME) Church and sent to Allen Chapel AME Church in Clearfield, Pennsylvania, one hour from my home. The presiding elder had a name of one of the leaders in the church and the church address. My wife and I went to Clearfield and met with Mr. Lonnie Moore, and we opened that little church back up. The seating capacity was forty, and we would regularly have a relatively packed house of thirty or more. I loved that little church, and they loved me. I stayed there until I got my doctorate in ministry, and then I was moved to my first full-time pastorate.

Ebenezer AME Church in Aliquippa, Pennsylvania, was my first full-time charge. This was a church that was famous for killing preachers. I followed Rev. William Estes, who had died of a heart attack reportedly suffered after a church board meeting. I remember Bishop Henry A. Belin saying to me as he gave me the appointment, "If you can pastor Ebenezer, you can pastor anywhere." I arrived with no fanfare and no welcoming committee. The fight began day one. They didn't like me, and I was trying to love them. I was young, arrogant, idealistic, broke, and preaching like crazy. The officers were upset when I required all potential and existing officers to meet with me prior to the new conference year to share with me their salvation story. If they weren't saved, then they couldn't serve. They were appalled at such an ultimatum. We are not even going to talk about my requiring leaders to attend some form of Bible study.

This was a difficult entrance. It wasn't a good move. It wasn't a good match. They weren't ready for me, and I wasn't ready to pastor them. Needless to say, the relationship did not last long. I was glad when Bishop Belin promoted me and moved me to the inner city of Pittsburgh, to a church that was fifteen minutes from my home.

Trinity AME Church in the Hill District of Pittsburgh, Pennsylvania, was my next church. I followed Rev. Wilfred Messiah, who would later be elected a bishop in our church. This church was ready for new leadership. Rev. Messiah and his wife, Mother Carolyn Messiah, had prepared the church for the transition. They had let the members know that their time was up and that new leadership was coming. They had prepared the congregation by teaching them, talking about transition, and making the difficult decisions so that the new pastor would not have to make those choices. The church had been renovated, given a new sound system, painted inside and out. All I had to do was to come and open the doors and continue to grow the church. This was a good marriage because the groundwork had been laid, the church was prepared, and it was a good fit. I am an inner-city guy who loves the street. While loving school and having become solidly upper-middle class, my roots are in the 'hood. This was a 'hood church—in and of the 'hood. This was me. We went together. The church experienced phenomenal growth spiritually, numerically, and financially. My predecessor let me pastor the people, and they gave me permission to lead them.

In the three short stories I have shared, you can see why I say that considering a new pastorate has both joys and pains. I don't think we can ever eliminate the emotional tension involved in pastoral transitions, but I do believe we can manage them. We can make moves better and smoother if we are intentional and learn what makes a move good. This book will walk you through what I and others have learned from experience, research, and the case studies included in the book. The goal is to make your transition manageable for you and for the church, with casualties on neither side. Change in pastoral leadership involves a lot of emotional work. The outgoing pastoral team and family, the incoming leadership, and the congregation are all involved in this conflicted emotional transition that is strange and in many ways undefined and unnamed—we don't seem to have a language to talk about it. Often, we really don't know how to feel about or how to navigate pastoral transitions.

I close with one more story—this one from my personal life. I remember when we were going through the final stages of adopting our son. We had prayed and fasted for God to send us a little boy. God answered our prayer and presented us with the boy of our dreams. Little Ralph was eighteen months old at the time and was staying with his foster parents, who loved him as much as we did. Although we were excited about God's blessing, Ralph's foster parents were losing the son we were gaining. I will never forget the day we met at the adoption agency for the transfer. They were bringing Ralph so that he could go home with us. As we were smiling and crying, Ralph's foster parents, too, were smiling and crying. We were collectively both happy and sad, not to mention what was going on inside Ralph. In that room on that day, we didn't know what or how to feel. We were emotionally unsettled while celebrating the moment of transition. I think pastoral transitions resemble that experience. They are moments of celebration surrounded by moments of intense emotion that can be managed but not ignored. Let's walk together as we think about pastoral transition in your life and in the life of your church.

Acknowledgments

I want to thank Rev. Brenda Gregg, Bishop Noel Jones, Rev. Otis Moss III, Rev. Dr. Frank A. Thomas, Rev. Dr. Leslie D. Callahan, and their congregations for sharing their stories with me.

|1|

New Leadership— Old Issues

Keys to Successful Pastoral Transitions

....

The whole congregation of the Israelites set out from Elim; and Israel came to the wilderness of Sin, which is between Elim and Sinai, on the fifteenth day of the second month after they had departed from the land of Egypt. The whole congregation of the Israelites complained against Moses and Aaron in the wilderness. (Exodus 16:1-2, NRSV)

....

Just six weeks after they had left Egypt, the Hebrew people began to grumble about their new leaders, Moses and Aaron. The exodus, which had begun with great drama and fanfare, soon deteriorated into murmurs and complaints. Ministry transitions today aren't much different. No matter how greatly anticipated the change, the question isn't really *if* dissatisfaction and opposition will arise; the question is *when*.

Pastoral transitions are tough; there's no way of escaping that. They are not just tough; they are inevitable. All churches eventually go through pastoral transition. However, as difficult as such transitions are, there are practical principles that can make the pain and complexities of these changes more

1

manageable. The task for church leaders today is to help the pastor and congregation alike navigate the challenges that arise in the midst of significant changes in leadership style, personality, and vision.

> A healthy pastoral transition is one that enables a church to move forward into the next phase of its external and internal development with a new leader appropriate to those developmental tasks, and with a minimum of spiritual, programmatic, material, and people losses during the transition.[1]

Perhaps more than any mainline church culture, churches in the African American community are facing massive pastoral transition. As we look at the African American church, what we find is that civil rights–era pastors are retiring, and the next generations are up to lead. Thus, African American churches are doing more than simply moving from one pastor to the next; in these transitions are generational-divide issues like never before. The bridge generation, those who are too young to be considered civil rights and too old to be hip-hop, have been the first to be elevated in the African American pulpit; and right behind them will be the hip-hop generation.

The tension for historic African American churches will be that of calling a pastor who doesn't reflect the elder-leadership ethos of African American culture. Leaders in our older churches probably grew up listening to rhythm and blues, while the new pastor may have grown up listening to P-funk or hip-hop. These music styles speak to a larger cultural divide—a divide where identity tends to be based more on class than race alone, where transparency is valued over piety, where personal history is as important as communal past, and where leaders are expected to be human and flawed, not heroic and held in awe.[2] This being the case, congregations must be strategic and intentional as we welcome the pastors who will lead our churches in the twenty-first century. Similarly, those pastors will need to recognize the generational divide and minister to it, while simultaneously building the church of the future. Love, respect, and a commitment to move intentionally in the direction of God's leading—these must be some of the foundational principles that guide ministries in these times of transition.

A Cautionary Tale of Transition: My Story, Your Story, Our Story

The *Los Angeles Times* announced on November 9, 2004: "New Pastor Named at First AME." The article went on to observe, "The Rev. John J. Hunter is praised as a strategic thinker and forceful civil rights advocate with a personable and conciliatory nature." The writer interviewed Bishop John Bryant, who appointed Pastor John to First AME, and said the bishop described Hunter as a "highly creative 'people person' who combines strong theological training and pastoral skills with a background in law, business management and community activism."[3]

Despite Bishop Bryant's endorsement of his choice, there was an undertone of skepticism as the article reported on the bishop's confidence that "Hunter could move from an 1,800-member Seattle congregation with a $4 million annual budget to the Los Angeles church, with 18,000 members, 15 affiliated nonprofit entities and a total budget of $15 million." Asked how Hunter reacted to his selection, Bryant said: "He leapt at the chance. He was excited about the challenge."[4]

If Pastor Hunter was excited, we might wonder if he was also on guard. After all, he was following a legend, Pastor Chip Murray, who had been beloved pastor and father to the First AME family and a highly regarded civic leader in the Los Angeles community for twenty-seven years. How would the congregation receive Hunter?

The issues of moving from one pastor to the next differ in kind and degree based on the type of pastor one follows, but there is a central issue: The new pastor is not the former pastor.

When a pastor follows a legend like Chip Murray, issues of change, allegiance, and pastoral relationship are amplified. Pastor Hunter not only was unlike Pastor Murray, but the two were polar opposites in many ways. Sometimes churches who call a pastor, and some bishops who appoint pastors think a congregation needs something different from the former pastor. In cases where the differences are polar opposites, it creates an even greater divide.

The early days of a pastorate are about trajectory. There is going to be some tension, but the plane has to get off the ground to get the journey started. Folk have to be strapped in until they reach a comfortable cruising altitude.

> That period of growing together, of interacting with one another, progressively learning from one another, is what I mean by "trajectory of ministry." The relationship retains a "liveliness" to it. . . . If that building process really happens, the ministry will take off. If it does not happen, in a year or two you won't see a trajectory with pastor and people growing. Instead you will see a flat line. . . . Often what happens, the relationship deteriorates and pretty soon people start taking potshots at each other and scapegoating one another.[5]

In the case of First AME, the early tension that adversely affected the pastor-congregation relational trajectory began in 2004 and was still present in 2009. A number of factors had affected the transition: the long-term pastor left the church, which almost always calls for some type of interim adjustment period; the appointment of a pastor who was in many ways the opposite of his predecessor; and the early decisions made by the new pastor that changed the identity of the institution in a manner that lingered for five years. The church was struggling to do the work necessary to put the past in perspective. The trajectory of the pastoral relationship had become stunted; the question became, had it flatlined?

Congregations *can* manage the change process of transitions. Congregations that thrive in transitions and ensure that the pastoral trajectory doesn't flatline, we have found, do nine things well.

Nine Traits of Successful Pastoral Transitions[6]

1. Honor, respect, and celebrate the past.
2. Maximize the church's strengths.
3. Complete the past.
4. Articulate the church's vision.
5. Develop a strategic plan.
6. Manage the dark side.
7. Commit to the long haul.
8. Do the work of ministry.
9. Listen to God's voice.

Honor, Respect, and Celebrate the Past

When we study the First AME transition, we can see the tension in the beginning. Let's look at what happened at First AME from the retirement of Pastor Murray to the coming of Pastor Hunter. The *Los Angeles Times*, September 18, 2004, stated, "The congregation doesn't want him to go. They had hoped the church's quadrennial AME conference in Indianapolis this June would extend the retirement age. Instead, the body reaffirmed it. And after months of saying no, the minister is finally ready to talk to a reporter about the R word."[7]

It didn't matter who was going to be appointed to this church, there were going to be issues. This is the case with every new pastor, but it was aggravated in this situation because of the circumstances, the appearance of a forced retirement, and who Pastor Hunter was following. Not only had the church fought the retirement, but also there was no real preparation for the transition. They hadn't done the work of closure. The church was in grief, and the grief took many forms. In transitions like this, the emotions must be identified and attended to as a pastor would in any grief situation.

When the new pastor comes, there is an identity crisis a church goes through as they ask who they are and who they will be in the future. In the African American church, the identity of the congregation is heavily linked to that of the pastor. As transitions are made, pastors and congregations must take stock of what these changes mean, how they are respected, and how they are negotiated. Pastors and congregations need to nurture each other through these periods as they are cognizant of this phase of transition and, therefore, intentionally navigate these murky conditions.

Honor the legacy of the church while not being held hostage to the past. As the congregation moves on and develops a relationship with their new pastor, they build on the healthy parts of the church that need to continue to be nurtured while simultaneously honoring and welcoming the new leadership. The new pastor must lead in respecting the legacy of his or her predecessor while being the pastor God has called him or her to be.

Maximize the Church's Strengths

When a congregation and its new pastor quickly identify the healthier parts of the church, they are empowered to strengthen what is already strong. When a new pastor enters the doors of the church, he or she must have a learning agenda. The new pastor must learn the history of the church and the present state of the church. Congregants, and especially leaders in a congregation, must work to educate their new leadership. This education doesn't take the form of "this is the way we have always done it." Instead, this education explains who the church has been and who it is, and says, "now we want to take our past and build on it for our future."

In the process of the transition, churches and pastoral teams have to deal with their strengths and weaknesses as they seek to define this new relationship. As the new pastoral team leads with the church, these relationships are worked out, strengths and weaknesses are discovered, as they focus on doing ministry together.

Complete the Past

A part of the work of transitions is completing the past. How does a congregation close the door on yesterday while opening the door to the future? The answer to this question isn't simple, and it can't be answered quickly, but it must be posed and talked about often. Congregations must place the issues of past, present, and future on the table and talk about them openly. They have to discuss what they want to become in partnership with their new pastor while not dismissing what they were under the former pastor's leadership.

The reality is that congregations, especially in the African American church, see the life of their church in the shadow of the tenure of a pastor. As transitions are made, pastors and congregations must take stock of what these markers mean, how they are respected, and how they are negotiated. Pastors and congregations need to nurture each other through these periods as they are cognizant of this phase of transition and, therefore, intentionally navigate these murky conditions.

In the case of First AME, Pastor John walked into a very delicate situation. When a pastor walks into such a powder keg of emotions during a transition, the decisions made in the early days are crucial. The new pastor has to focus on developing relationships and dealing with the grief the church is going through. The new pastor must realize that the congregation's grief doesn't necessarily mean they don't want the new pastor, but they are grieving the loss of the relationship that they had with the former pastor.

Articulate the Church's Vision

After bringing closure to the past, the church moves toward the future with a clear picture of what it is becoming. The new pastor has to lead in vision casting. As the new pastor leads, the leaders and the church have to run with and inform that vision. Informing the vision is best done by working hard to welcome the new pastoral team, to work with them, to talk with them, to build a healthy relationship with them, and to dream together. Vision isn't a top-down thing that God zaps preachers with. Vision comes from God to God's people. Many times it is spoken through the pastor, and the people or the congregation are also a part of this conversation. The reason vision is so essential is that, as a church moves on, they have to know where they are going. When a church does not have clear vision of the future, they will not complete the work of the past. Where there is no vision, a church gets lost in the wilderness.

Develop a Strategic Plan

The pastor will lead the strategic planning process, which in turn equips the church to realize God's vision. This is the work of capacity building, of equipping the church for its future. Without a plan, the vision is empty. As a church articulates vision, they then must structure, restructure, and equip the church to accomplish the vision. This may mean getting rid of some things, stopping some things, starting new things, and doing more of what the church already has been doing. This is where real change comes in to play. For a church to become something new, it is going to have to change. A church and new pastor who are clear about the essential changes they have to make do well in transitions because they understand what those changes are, why they have to make them, and how those changes will bring them in line with God's vision for their church.

In the case of First AME, Pastor Hunter came in and made some staffing changes that he obviously felt were necessary, but they upset some in the congregation. This is normal in transitions, and new pastors have to be wise about making major decisions early on in their tenure. There can be a grace period extended to new pastors when major decisions can be made with congregational support. If such a period is extended, one has to be strategic and wise in how one uses that capital. If major decisions are made early, without sufficient information or sensitivity to history and relationships, these decisions could extend the transition period or be the cause for a failed or intensified transition. When in a transition, one must do the right thing and make the right decisions, but this cannot be done without a sense of godly wisdom and timing. Pastors have to make decisions about staffing and the direction of the church, but it's important to be clear about whether a decision must be made immediately and when a decision can wait.

Manage the Dark Side

Pastors must define their own strengths and weaknesses, building on their strengths and managing their weaknesses. They must also do this for the church. A part of leadership's responsibility is to define reality. We have to name what we really are and announce if the emperor doesn't have on any clothes.

For example, the role of the pastor's spouse is a central issue in the African American church. Gender roles play a big part in the life of the African American church, and in many cases shades of sexism inform these role expectations. Pastor Hunter brought his highly competent wife in as leader of First AME Renaissance, the church's economic development arm, thus giving Mrs. Denise Hunter a leadership role, a contrast with Pastor Murray's wife, whose role had been stereotypical. This decision increased tensions, criticism, and distance in the relationship that Mrs. Hunter would have with some of the leaders of the church. She would not be the stereotypical missionary leader. Mrs. Hunter was a young professional woman with two grown daughters and a six-year-old daughter at home. She brought a different swagger to the position of church leader and pastor's wife.

The role that the spouse played prior to the new pastor and the way roles will be defined in a tenure change are also a key concern for the African American church. As first families come into the life of a church, they must be mindful of what they are following, aware of the definition and expectations of the role of first family. If they are going to have a radically different role from what the church has had and therefore expects, they must intentionally lay the groundwork that redefines that role. They are changing the first-family norms, and this can't be done without respect for what those norms were in the past.

Commit to the Long Haul

Transitions are difficult, painful, and time-consuming. People have to give a pastor permission to pastor them. New pastors must realize that, while they have the title, they have to establish the relationship. Pastors who succeed are committed to the relationship. They work at it; they nurture it. They intentionally love the people, and the people will love them back. Churches that succeed in transitions learn to love their new pastor, while not disparaging their former pastor. They buy into the fact that building a new relationship takes hard work and long hours. They can't quit when the going gets tough. As churches and pastors fight through together, their shared experience strengthens the relationship.

What I have found in my research is that the key to successful transitions in pastoral leadership is accepting that the church is in a period of transition and that there is no choice but to move forward. Moving forward can mean many things, but the fact is that a church can't go back to yesterday. This statement sounds simple, but it is profound in its simplicity. Successful transitions are like going on a journey: You have to get started; and, when you get started, there comes a point of no return.

The process and time it takes to move from what was to what is and what will be is just that—a process. Transitions take time. Pastors and congregations have to be committed to this process for the long haul. The transition process doesn't happen overnight. It is commonly accepted that it takes seven years at a minimum for the transition from one pastoral team to another pastoral team truly becoming pastor.

Do the Work of Ministry

The work of ministry is the common bond between the new pastor and the church. As they labor together in love, in the work of kingdom building, the labor brings them together. Churches that do well in transition focus on doing ministry. They focus primarily on the five things the church does: worship, fellowship, spiritual care and nurture, education, and outreach and service. During times of transition, a church must be intentionally mission focused. While they have to minister to the transition and the pain of inevitable loss, they must still focus on the essentials of being the church of Jesus Christ. This focus will grow the congregation as a spiritually mature people who will hear from God and follow God and God's plan for their future.

In the midst of transition, issues can arise that can take the church's eyes off of ministry, and they can become distracted by side issues, personality conflicts, congregational splits, and fights. What focuses churches is a compelling vision, with leadership that leads them in doing the work of the ministry for the glory of God. This may sound a bit trite and idealistic, but I will argue that if a church isn't about ministry, it is about mess. When churches are about mess in the midst of a transition, the messier the transition becomes. The messier the transition, the greater the opportunity for the transition and the ministry to be derailed altogether.

Listen to God's Voice

God's call and confirmation of that call speaks louder than the minority of critics and naysayers. Churches and church leaders who hear the voice of God in the midst of the transition are the ones that succeed. This means the church spends time in prayer and studying God's Word. They come to church not *in*specting but expecting. They know that they—pastor and congregation—are poised to hear from God.

When the focus is the doing ministry and listening to God's voice about where God wants to take the congregation, the congregation and the new pastoral team have less time for mess. To focus the transition, the church has to lift up ministry by focusing on worship, fellowship, nurturing, education, outreach and service. The church has to wrestle with how they can be faithful to serving God by witnessing within and outside the four walls of the church. Some of their questions should focus them to think about the norms of behavior. How do we handle ourselves in the transition? How do we have civil conversations about change? How do we embrace and respect where we are going versus where we have been? What private conversations are to be kept within the congregation, and what subjects do we talk about outside the church?

Every church will go through pastoral transitions. The question is how will each church manage the transition?

Reflection Questions

1. How will we move on from where we are to where God wants us to be?
2. What is our dark side?
3. What are our strengths?

4. What are the major issues that a new pastor would have to deal with in our church?

5. How do we know we are ready to move on to what God has for us in the future?

NOTES

1. Carolyn Weese and J. Russell Crabtree, *The Elephant in the Boardroom: Speaking the Unspoken about Pastoral Transitions* (San Francisco: Jossey-Bass, 2004), 41.

2. I explore this cultural divide extensively in *The Gospel Remix: Reaching the Hip Hop Generation* (Judson Press, 2008), a book I coauthored with Jason A. Barr Jr., Jamal-Harrison Bryant, William H. Curtis, and Otis Moss III.

3. Teresa Watanabe, "New Pastor Named at First AME; The Rev. John J. Hunter is praised as a strategic thinker and forceful civil rights advocate with a personable and conciliatory nature," *Los Angeles Times*, November 9, 2004.

4. Ibid.

5. Loren B. Mead, *A Change of Pastors . . . and How it Affects Change in the Congregation* (Herndon, VA: Alban Institute, 2005), 13–14.

6. Adapted from Weese and Crabtree, *Elephant in the Boardroom*, 15–27. These nine points are extrapolated from their six principles.

7. Gayle Pollard-Terry, "A Lion in Winter," *Los Angeles Times*, September 18, 2004.

|2|

It Ain't Just
about the Pastor

A Team Approach to Transition

····

What then is Apollos? And what is Paul? Servants through whom you came to believe, as the Lord assigned to each. I planted, Apollos watered, but God gave the growth. So neither the one who plants nor the one who waters is anything, but only God who gives the growth. The one who plants and the one who waters have a common purpose, and each will receive wages according to the labor of each. For we are God's servants, working together; you are God's field, God's building.

According to the grace of God given to me, like a skilled master builder I laid a foundation, and someone else is building on it. Each builder must choose with care how to build on it. (1 Corinthians 3:5-10, NRSV)

····

Planning for the Inevitable

Pastoral transitions are not moments in time marked merely by first sermons or installation services. Pastoral transitions are about journeying together as one pastor leaves and a new pastor and his or her family come to be a part of their new church family. But, the journey begins weeks or months before the new pastor arrives:

[F]rom the moment you discover your pastor is leaving until well after the new pastor is in place, you are journeying toward that common commitment to new life and new mission. You are not in a "hiring process." You are in a transformation process. You will be transformed and your new pastor will be transformed.[1]

Pastoral transitions are transformations, and these transformations cannot be done successfully without all parties being active participants in the process. Congregations should not feel *acted upon* when they receive the new pastor, but they should be active participants in this journey. While some congregations may feel disempowered in the transition process, the arrival of the new pastoral family offers new and creative opportunities for the congregation to become proactive instead of reactive—by playing an integral role in making the transition as smooth as possible.

Even as every pastor begins as a visitor, remember also that every arriving pastor will one day be a departing pastor. Pastors are strangers in a congregation that, in essence, they come to leave. The reality of pastoral ministry is that every pastor will leave a church through retirement, moving to another congregation, resignation or, God forbid, some tragedy. Members, on the other hand, tend to stay at their churches. Generally, members don't join churches expecting that one day they will be moving on; most members come to stay.

Since a part of the reality of pastoral ministry is transition, congregations need to be mindful at the beginning of the relationship that transition is a part of the relationship, and they should always be mindful and be prepared for the inevitable. "[E]very pastor is a departing pastor, the day to begin thinking about a transition play is the day the [new] pastor arrives. This forces the pastor to think strategically, to reflect on what he or she wants to accomplish in his or her ministry, what he or she wants to offer as a base for his or her successor to build on."[2]

Churches have to develop in the present as they build for the future. The church then adopts the new pastor, while building on what was, and developing for the future reality of transition. This may seem contradictory, but it is much like having a new child and while simultaneously starting to save for a college fund. This child will have to leave one day, becoming a mature young adult.

As a pastoral family enters the life of a congregation, the congregation should adopt that pastoral family and make them a part of the larger church family. When any family gains a new member, there are going to be issues. I remember when our second child, Nicole, was born. Nicole hadn't done anything to our firstborn, Nastasia, except show up. While Nicole, newly arrived from the hospital, quietly slept on the couch, Nastasia—all of one year old—walked by and just hit her little sister. It took some time for Nastasia to welcome Nicole into the family. Vanessa and I had to work hard to make them see that we are family. Over time, these little girls grew together and loved each other and learned to be happy as sisters. (In their early twenties now, they are the best of friends.)

Like parents introducing a new child to older siblings, the leaders of the church have to do the work of intentionally integrating a newly arrived pastor into the life of the congregation. This integration process has to be outlined with some sense of being methodical. It can't be willy-nilly. Part of the transition plan should include these questions:

- Whom does the pastor need to meet?
- What ministries or relationships does the pastor need to focus on in those early months?
- What issues are brewing in the congregation that the pastor needs to know about right away?
- What issues and areas can wait?

When churches experience a pastoral transition, that transition isn't just about the pastor and his or her family. The entire body is going through transition, and for this to work well there must be a team approach to the transition. Folk need to realize that it is in the best interest of everybody involved for the transition to go well. It is even in the best interest of the former pastoral family that the transition go well. All of the hard work the previous pastoral family did for the church should be honored. When transitions don't go well, what was built up is torn down, and the labors of the previous leadership, who worked so hard in the church, are essentially for naught. Transforming a church demands hard work from the lay leadership of the church as well as from the pastoral family. Thus, when a new pastor comes in, you don't want to lose that momentum or squander what has been accomplished.

Invest in the transition, and see it as a team effort that benefits everyone. To do this right, there must be a team approach to the transition process. No one wins when transitions don't go well. There are forces in churches that line up and stand against the new pastor. They have a vested interest in this battle, but in the end no one wins when posses in the congregation take a stand against the new pastor. A team approach means we invest in those tangible acts that make a positive difference in the transition. We don't take sides; we don't engage in fights that produce stalemates. We commit to talking through the issues of the transitions; we keep our cards on the table and deal with issues in the appropriate forums.

Cementing the New Relationship

Congregational leaders must guard against the temptation to take sides in a pastoral transition. In some cases, members will be committed to the former pastor. They have been pastored by the former minister and often have loving relationships with that person. It is hard to embrace a new person in the role of the former, but congregations have to wrestle with how this can be done. A congregation must ask how they can move forward in solidifying a relationship with the new pastoral family. The development of a quality relationship with the new pastoral family is difficult, it is hard work, but congregations and new pastoral families are to understand that this is part of the process. Don't be put off by the tension the new relationship brings; tension is normal, and if the congregation takes time to review its history, this same type of tension may have been present when the preceding pastor came. One of the keys in this new relationship is giving it a chance to succeed while realizing there is going to be some tension in the early going.

A guiding principle in these early days of the relationship is love. Congregants and the new pastoral family must extend the active ethic of loving each other. It is almost like an early dating relationship, if you will pardon my metaphor. In those early days of dating, we spend a lot of time with each other just talking and being together. This very simple but powerful approach of talking, listening, and doing nice things for each other can go a long way. The approach goes both ways: pastors have to make themselves available to the people and allow them to get to know them.

When a new pastor comes to visit (which is what they are doing, even when they have been appointed or called by the congregation), the new pastor *must* realize this when the courting officially begins. When we court, we dress up and put our best foot forward. Both the pastor and the congregation will do this at first. It takes time to trust and open up, so the new pastor and congregation must take it slow, but be intentional about the road they are going down. Commit to making this relationship work, keeping in mind the covenant that has been made. The church is adopting the new pastor and his or her family.

A pastor who feels genuinely welcomed by and in the congregation is in a better position to serve that congregation. Simply put, this is the goal of the church's hospitality—the pastor's adoption into the church's life and ministry. It is important, therefore, that the church learn how not only to welcome the new pastor but to live with whatever level of uncertainty or insecurity his or her presence brings to the new situation.[3] During those first few months and even years, there is an uncertainty in what this new pastoral relationship will mean for the pastor, the congregation, and the community. Congregations and pastors have to name this as a part of the reality, and both have to find ways to put the other at ease. Openness, transparency, and intensifying the relationship during those early months are important.

During these first few months, there is this feeling out process; boundary work is being done, which delineates the expectations of the pew and the pulpit as well as the lines between what is private and what is shared. The pastor and the congregation are trying to negotiate this new relationship that is caught up in areas of responsibility and authority. Who had the power to do what, and who will now have the power is a part of this boundary work. How far can we go? How far should we go? This boundary work is also being negotiated in the context of intense relational work.

Adopting the New Family

When churches call a new pastor, they have to understand that they aren't contracting a hired hand or a freelance leader. Rather, they are inviting the pastoral family to become part of their community. They are calling the pastoral family in to live with them.

The first job of the congregation is to welcome the new pastor and his or her family. This welcome isn't merely the welcoming event on the inaugural Sunday, but it is a constant outreach process during those first few months and into the first few years. Congregations might plan a yearlong welcome itinerary for the new pastoral family, an itinerary that will be sensitive to their need to transition into a new life and perhaps into a new city or region of the country. Anyone who has made a major household move knows that the demands of such a life transition are stressful and far-reaching.

As congregational leaders, it is important to begin this process by asking some basic questions:

- What do newcomers need to know upon arriving in a new place? Consider practical and mundane information such as the locations of local grocery stores, gas stations, health-care providers, schools, and entertainment centers. Provide a folder with important addresses, emergency numbers, and public transportation schedules. Include a local map that is marked with key locations. Be sure to provide brochures for local businesses, and include the take-out menus from a few favorite restaurants!

- Will the newcomers be prepared for their new home's typical weather? Perhaps provide a survival kit suited to the church's region—for example, umbrellas and rain ponchos for Seattle; brimmed hats and sunscreen for Phoenix and Atlanta; mosquito repellent and information about hurricane preparations in Miami; and warm gloves, scarves, and a snow shovel for Chicago.

- If the pastoral family includes children, what are their ages and genders? Consider a different kind of survival kit for the parents—include some age-appropriate toys or games to keep the kids occupied while parents unpack, the phone numbers and references for babysitters in the congregation or community, a map marked with playgrounds and parks, or brochures from local businesses with child-friendly activities.

- Then consider how the congregation can offer regular events or other gestures that are a visible sign of welcome for the new pastoral family. Perhaps plan monthly dinners sponsored by different church ministries, inviting the pastor and family as honored guests. At these dinners, the ministry leaders could share their personal stories and the stories of their ministries. The pastoral family in return could share their story. Hearing one another's stories is vital to the transformation of *mine* and *theirs* into a shared *ours* as a new story develops in the life of the congregation.

As the congregation thinks about welcoming the new pastor, there are several questions they could ask themselves as they prepare to make the new pastoral family feel at home:

1. How can we make our new pastoral family feel welcomed throughout their first year with us?
2. What can we do monthly that would make the family feel welcomed?
3. How can we get to know them, and how can we make sure they get to know us?
4. What will they need to make their transition into the life of our congregation smoother?
5. When and how can we help protect their family time during the transition?
6. How can we find out what they need?
7. What would we need if we were moving into a new city and a new church?
8. What can we do, not just for the pastor, but for each member of the pastoral family to make sure he or she feels welcomed?
9. How shall we ensure that some member(s) of the congregation are praying daily for our pastoral family?

Teaching the New Pastor the History of the Church

For the transition process to work, the pastor will have to be brought up to date on the history of the church. The pastor must be a student in the early days, listening and not judging the past, so he or she can build on that legacy. Even in churches that are struggling to survive, the new pastor has to respect the fact that the congregation has survived to this point, and he or she has someone to lead and to love as the people of

God. In too many instances, new pastors come in and don't have a full appreciation for the past. There is this sense in some circles that the new pastor must erase the predecessor's legacy. This attitude is not only disrespectful to the people and the former pastor, it is also disrespectful to God. The new pastor has to respect what God has done in that congregation.

Respecting the past is also relevant when a pastor inherits a ministry that is thriving. To try and wipe out the legacy of one's predecessor isn't biblical. Pastors have to recognize that no matter the condition in which they find a church, they are building on a legacy. If the legacy is a firm foundation, celebrate it, expand it, and inquire about how this legacy should inform the future direction of the church. This means that is important to talk with the congregation respectfully as to what that legacy is, invite the congregation to assess what they built with the former pastor, the good and the bad. The new pastor has to be cautious in this conversation, because he or she is new in this family and may not have earned the right to be critical as of yet. The new pastor has to remember when he or she criticizes a church's past, be it the former pastor or the present condition of the church, he or she is talking about the very people to whom he or she is speaking. Paul put it this way, "Be careful how you build."

In his first letter to the Corinthians, the apostle Paul alludes to some principles that should inform pastoral transitions when he talks about respecting the past and being careful on how a pastor builds on what he or she inherits. As we reflect on the team approach in pastoral transitions, note that in the context of biblical passage quoted at the beginning of the chapter, divided loyalties among the believers at Corinth were fueling fights in the church. Among the potential behaviors during the transition period, some (such as squabbles over leader loyalty) prove to be less than helpful in moving the process along.

When a congregation experiences transition, it is caught in this strange place of looking forward from the back seat. What do I mean by this? The past is part of the congregation's story. The new pastor doesn't know this story and in most cases wasn't a part of that story. He or she is now being called upon to share the driver's seat with the leadership team of the church. The pastor is asked to lead while still trying to assimilate the history or stories of the church. A pastor can't build carefully if he or she doesn't know, understand, or appreciate the foundation, the history of the church. The role of that church in the larger community is a part of this history.

The congregation can help the pastor understand how the church was started, so that, together, they can move forward. What did each pastoral leadership period give to the life of the church? The pros and cons of each pastoral administration should be scrutinized and reviewed.

We talked earlier about the congregation and the new pastor making it a part of the welcoming year to share the history. Documents, pictures, old annual reports, newspaper articles, key videos, and sermons of the former pastor could be assembled in a package for the new pastor. The church historian (official or unofficial) needs to have some significant time with the pastor as they systematically, from the beginning of the church history to the present, go through the story. In this way, the congregation can empower the new pastor to drive while at the same time saying, "We know these roads."

The delicate balance of submitting to leadership that by definition is naive about the history of the church's situation is tenuous at best. On the one hand, the pastor has to confess his or her lack of knowledge about the history of the church that he or she is called to build upon. On the other hand, the congregation has to empower the pastor as their new leader with this knowledge in a way that is respectful of his or her call to be their pastor, and not ask him to lead as the former pastors have led nor to lead in the same direction. There is this tension of where we have traveled and where we will travel. While the congregation historians have that knowledge of the old roads, they now have to look to new roads, new directions, and a journey that has yet to defined.

So how does a church and a new pastor deal with this delicate balance of front seat and back seat? Talk about it. The congregation can't be caught in the constant call of, "When Reverend So-and-So was the pastor, we did it this way." On the other hand, there are times when a new pastor would benefit greatly from the perspective of one who has driven the road before, who knows the shortcuts that are likely to get him lost or the detours necessary because a bridge is out ahead.

These are the roads we are talking about. The pastor will need the local guides in the church, but those who are guiding have to remember that they are asking the new pastor to drive, to lead the church. The reason for sharing about the old roads is to help the new pastor discover the new roads. Along the journey, the pastor is becoming the guide. "Your history can block your future, or it can blaze the trail for your future."[4] The new pastor and the church have to talk about the old landmarks, have to talk about the past, but not to be held hostage to that past. They must talk about them in a way to point the church toward the new landmarks. Old roads take us to the places we have been before; new roads take us to places God wants us to discover.

Who are we together, pastor and congregation? This is the new identity question. When a new pastor arrives, the church has to ask this question of who are we in the context of this new relationship and new time and space. Mead put it this way:

> This simply means getting a new fix on what is going on in the community in which this local church is geographically located. Just as congregations need to see how its membership has shifted and changed since it last formed its identity, even so the sense of identity of the community needs to be rethought.[5]

While the church looks back and reflects on its past, it can't stay parked there. The church and their new pastor have to ask new questions. What type of church are we being called to be today? What are our new socioeconomic and demographic realities, both internally and externally? A church can't be what they were under the former pastor. This is a new day that starts a new journey when the new pastor arrives.

Earning Cultural Capital

Church leaders have to help their new pastor get a working understanding of the culture of the church and community he or she needs to become an effective, informed leader. A newly arrived pastor is not a leader yet; remember he or she is merely a visitor. The pastor will become the leader only over time.

> There is a critical role that you as a congregation must play if your pastor is to gain the kind of cultural capital that the church knows and regards as worthy. *Cultural capital* refers to those particular elements of power and influence anchored in the congregation's own culture (stuff, sayings, and especially submerged beliefs) that persons and groups can acquire and use as they become accepted and trusted.[6]

The pastor has to know how to navigate the waters of the congregation so that he or she can lead the change process with the church leaders. The pastor will not know what the congregation doesn't tell him or her. "Cultural capital is closely tied to pastoral adoption. Without the pastor gaining sufficient and appropriate cultural capital, your church's pastoral ministry is in jeopardy."[7] Churches and pastors want this new relationship to succeed. The pain of a failed pastoral transition leaves carnage all over the church and community. As new leaders come in, they can learn from Barnabas. In Acts 9:26-30, it was Barnabas who vouched for Paul. The folk didn't quite know how they felt about Paul, but Barnabas, a respected leader in that community, stood with Paul, and his support gave Paul an opportunity to share and lead as he showed himself to the people. Leaders in the church have to sit with the new pastor and present him or her to the congregation. They, like Barnabas, have to "ride with" the pastor during the transition.

The reality is that a new pastor is not the pastor because he or she was called or appointed to the church; title does not equal relationship. As the new pastor connects with the people, serves the people, loves the people, he or she earns the title in the eyes of the congregation. "A pastor's ability to get something done or to make something happen depends in large part upon the congregation's acceptance, trust, and respect."[8]

Practically speaking, what steps might a pastor take to earn a congregation's acceptance? How does a pastor gain a congregation's trust? How does a pastor warrant their respect? These are lessons I have learned through my own experiences with pastoral transition.

1. PRESENCE

A pastor must be present and accounted for in the relationship. Absentee pastors will not have the quality and quantity of time needed to learn the congregation. As a pastor becomes a part of the congregation, the pastor must guard his or her schedule to make time for congregants. The community will call, denominational loyalties will call, but for the first year or so of ministry, the priority must lie in being active in the life of the church by being present and actively engaging in developing this new relationship.

This may mean that there will be an imbalance during that first year as the pastor focuses on building a relationship with the congregation. The pastor has to schedule time to be with members (events, annual days); visit the older saints; conduct funerals, weddings, and baptisms; offer counseling; touch the people before and after worship. This is intense relationship work that can't be done if the pastor is absent. This is emotional work that takes time and energy. There are no short-cuts; there are no substitutions for the pastor's consistent and engaged presence.

2. PREACHING AND WORSHIP

New pastors must make preaching a priority. A key role of the shepherd of any flock is feeding the flock. If a new pastor goes into a situation where the pulpit has been shared by associates or annual day speakers, that practice needs to be reconsidered, especially for the first year. The new pastor should be the lead preacher and should have the right to decide who preaches and when. Old practices may be restored if the pastor is led in that direction, but at least during that first year, the new pastor needs to preach as many Sundays as he or she can handle. As the pastor makes preaching a priority, the congregation must give him or her time to prepare. Study and preparation are critical to quality preaching. The pastor who is overbooked and doesn't have time to prepare will not be able preach effectively. In the African American tradition, preaching is central to the role and duties of our pastors. We expect a well-prepared word and a word that is delivered well. The new pastor needs to be present in worship from invocation to benediction. Once a pastor learns a church, coming into the pulpit after worship has started is acceptable. During that first year, a key to getting to know the people is to fully worship with them as a worshipping pastor.

3. TEACHING

New pastors must take time to teach God's Word outside of the Sunday worship experience. The weekly Bible study is not just about the Word of God; it is also about relationships. Bible study tends to be a much smaller group than most churches see on Sunday. It is a time for the pastor to touch the people outside the pressures of Sunday and get to know them. This act of relationship-building leads to the new pastor caring for the people, praying with them, visiting them, and walking with them through their good times and bad times. In addition to Bible study, the pastor can also think about other teaching moments. Pastors can visit choir rehearsals and ministry meetings and share a word. Teaching isn't just relegated to Bible study; the principle is that a new pastor must teach.

4. PASTORAL CARE

During that first year, the relationship between the pastor and the congregation will intensify through intentional acts of love manifested via pastoral care. Pastoral care is simply caring for the people: calling and seeing about the people in times of tragedy, celebrating with the people in times of joy. New pastors have to show the congregation that they care. It is one thing for a pastor to have a good heart and quite another for that pastor to let folk know he or she loves them. When a congregation knows that their new pastor loves them, and that pastor has shown that love through tangible acts of caring, it will go a long way in moving the transition along. The new pastor has to remember that what makes the former pastor's legacy so long is relationship.

5. ORGANIZATION AND ADMINISTRATION

The new pastor must be brought up to speed on where the organizational structure of the church is and where it is going. People are looking to the pastor to lead and order the church. A new pastor must first know what was and what is, and then must decide with his or her leaders what ought to be. A good administrator is not birthed, but rather is made by paying attention to what is going on, seeking answers to questions, and sharing leadership with knowledgeable people who can cover the new pastor's weaknesses and make the work of the ministry happen. The new pastor has to balance the administrative task of the church in such a way that it points the church toward its future.

6. LEAVE THE OLD CHURCH BEHIND

As pastor of a new church, he or she must accept that he or she isn't the pastor at the old church anymore. A minister can't pastor two churches. The new pastor has to pour his or her energies into the new congregation. Let the old church go. Don't take calls or entertain complaints about the successor. Don't go back and do funerals. At some point, the new pastor needs to walk with the members through times of grief as part of pastoral care. I would add, be cautious about weddings, but I wouldn't rule them out. The principle here is simple: move on, and let the people go, and help them move on. A pastor can't move on and the former congregation can't move on if the pastor doesn't move out.

Loving the Old Pastor and Falling in Love with the New Pastor

Churches shouldn't have to choose whom to love. Congregations can't be asked to forget the former pastor, forget where he or she led them, and how he or she cared for them. The name of the former pastor can't be an anathema. The love for the former pastor should be enshrined while the congregation falls in love with the new pastor. The congregation can love both the former and the new pastor, but these relationships have to be managed as the church moves forward.

As the new pastor truly becomes the pastor, it is important for the congregation not to reach back. If the former pastor calls to inquire about how it is going with the church, members have to remind the pastor that he or she has moved on, and it isn't his or her business how the church is doing. Members have to turn to the new pastor.

For example, don't call the old pastor and ask him or her to do funerals. Call on the new pastor. As tempting as it is to fall back on that old relationship, be mindful that it isn't fair to the former pastor or current pastor. Feel free to invite the former pastor to a funeral, but the officiant—and in most cases, the eulogist—should be the present pastor. Of course, there are exceptions to any rule, and this is far from law; however, I have observed that when the new pastor is allowed to care for members during times of grief, it helps a church move forward. When the new pastor takes up the pastoral-care function, especially during times of grief, the relationship changes, deepens, grows more intimate. Ironically, grieving for the loved one brings the new pastor and congregation together and forces them to face a new future without that person they loved.

This change can also be likened to the pastoral transition itself. In many cases we lose the pastor we love, and it is as if he or she is now dead to us. In this process, churches must grieve, and the grieving process has to be led by the new pastor. He or she needs to take the church through the grieving process and help them move on to that new place in their pastoral relationship.

As the new pastor walks through the grieving process with the people, he or she will learn of their hurts, dreams, and desires. It is in the context of this new relationship that the pastor and the congregation will begin to see the future. The vision that God gives a pastor isn't the sole property or revelation of the pastor. "The vision the pastor articulates is not an arbitrary thing. It is a vision that arises out of two foci: the biblical message and the needs/dreams/hurts/visions of the people."[9]

As the pastor walks with the people, the vision will arise. The people need to see what they are going to look like with this new pastor. How will they live without the former pastor? How will the church be different? Where is the church going? Will it survive? The people are asking how the church will make it, and vision gives them the answer. A vision is not something that is spoken, but rather it something that is lived. The pastor and leadership team must speak to these insecurities as they focus on caring for the congregation and tenderly walking with them to the future. There is new life in this congregation. "We die to live, let us look and live," has to be the message in the transition.

Dealing with Conflict

In his first letter to the Corinthians, Paul is pointing out that behaviors that result in fighting, taking sides, or all-out church brawls aren't effective in a transition period. There are going to be differences and disagreements. How does a church deal with this reality? How do the new pastor, the leadership of the church, and the members voice their differences without making one another targets in the process? Small self-appointed committees that are focused on having their way (or having it the way things used to be) do not best serve the congregation's future. Their attempts to start fights are not healthy ways of dealing with tension in the transition.

On the flipside is the committee that is not self-appointed but is recruited by the pastor to be his or her battle force. No matter which individual or group initiates this hostile behavior, the result is exacerbation of the pain of transition. The proverbial salt in the wounds of change are neither healthy nor helpful. We have to remember that God is not the author of confusion. Tensions and disagreements are part of the transition process. The issue is how to articulate these issues in the open and not behind closed doors, on Internet blogs, or in the local press.

What is the right way to bring issues to the table? Every congregation must have a forum for conversation and must confront the tension of transition. If the church has an official board, deacon board, or church council, make it a point in the midst of transition to talk about the issues and pain of the transition. If the normal church polity doesn't allow for open dialogue in the transition process, a system may have to be developed. Small focus groups for conversation could be established. If the tension is such that the pastor or church leaders are not able to facilitate these conversations, then outside facilitators should be engaged to help move the congregation forward.

Churches and pastors can't pretend that there isn't pain in the transition. It is all right to have tension in the transition; name it and deal with it. Make it a regular agenda item to name what is going on in the transition and to ask how the church will resolve these issues so that the pastor and the church can continue to grow in and through the transition and become a healthy church family. The issues are brought to the table not to divide the church but to bring to light what issues are roaming around in the church that could derail the transition process if not dealt with properly, openly, and prayerfully.

During these trying and painful times, pray and seek God; focus on doing those things that bring the church to points of reconciliation and discourage behavior that is divisive. As churches reflect on how they might process these moments of tension, they can consider the following:

- Leaders, whose side are you on? Are you on God's side? Are you doing God's will?
- How will my action lead to resolution and reconciliation?
- Why I am bringing these issues to the table?
- What might be some stylistic issues regarding the new leadership style of our new pastor?
- Pastors, how do you want this church to treat you— like your former church did or like they treated their former pastor? How can you change the old patterns?
- Are you tempted to develop a battle group for your own defense? How is that destructive?
- To what extent does the church have a sense of direction? To what extent might the fighting be a result of the being lost or feeling lost?
- What is really going on here? What underlying issues might be at the root of the conflict?

Taking a Biblical Approach

The transition process calls for spiritual discernment, which means that dealing with these issues will not bring greater dissension but will bring the leadership team and congregation together. For resolution to occur, churches have to respond biblically. I have heard in many a church meeting, "Reverend, I was thinking . . ." or "The people are saying . . ." We have to ask instead, what does the Bible say? How does the Bible instruct us to lead and move forward? The Bible must be the guide in these conversations.

For example, Matthew 18:15-9 gives us principles to inform how we handle disputes and disagreements. The passage instructs us to go to that person and address the problem. If the person doesn't listen, we take someone with us and try again. If the other party still doesn't listen, then we take the matter up with the appropriate body in the church—but only after we have spoken to that person individually and with an objective witness. No one, neither member nor pastor, should be surprised in a large meeting by confrontation with the issues someone else has. Churches should follow the Matthew 18 principle in times of transition. Talk to each other, member to member, member to pastor, pastor to member, pastor and church leaders to members. Put the issues of offense on the table. When people fail to communicate with each other, misunderstanding runs rampant.

Avoiding the Pitfalls of Pastoral Pedestals

If we return to the 1 Corinthians passage, congregations are reminded that while we love those who lead us and have led us, a church does not belong to a single leader. Pastors, the church doesn't belong to you! We all belong to God. In the African American church, we have historically put our pastors on a sacred pedestal. They were the ones we empowered to lead us and fight for us. Our pastors were the ones who were well trained and were held in high esteem in our community. The beauty and grace of this relationship has served our community well.

The downside of this esteemed relationship is that, in some cases, the pastor and the identity of the church become synonymous. When the church becomes a pastoral personality cult, the result is a breeding ground for disillusion and destruction. When pastoral transition occurs in such a context, the necessary changes are made a hundred times more difficult. When God calls a church to accept a new leader, it is often because God desires to lead that community of faith in new directions. This may require a new congregational identity, a new mission statement, a new vision for the gospel ministry. That transition compels the church members as well as the new leadership to ask prayerfully, "God, who are we, and what is it you want us to become? We realize we don't belong to a pastor, and we are not limited to the identity of a pastor. God, we belong to you and we seek your guidance as we find out who we are to become in this time and in this place."

The richness of the African American pastoral tradition has been rooted in the loyal connection of pastor to congregation. Once again this is a product of our history. Our pastors have led every movement to come out of the African American community. These movements go back to our earliest times in America. It was our religious leaders who gave their all for our freedom from the evils of slavery. If we fast-forward to the twentieth century, we once again see it in the civil rights–era pastors who put their lives on the line for our freedom movements.

The twenty-first century will bring the same need for strong leadership. Our pastors are the ones who will sacrifice for us. They are the ones who care dearly for us. Our freedom leaders have a special bond with the congregation as a result of this history. When it is time for a transition form one pastor to the next, we can only expect that old loyalties will remain, and rightly so, as a result of this unique bond we form with our pastors during their tenure as our leaders. The question becomes, how do we move on—honoring old loyalties while building new ones? How do we avoid forming camps that result in division and could even bring disaster in the life of a congregation?

Avoiding the Camp Mentality

When transitions occur, there is the natural tendency to fall back into camps. The camp that was closest to the former pastor stands to lose the most. They were insiders, and now they stand to become outsiders. The fundamental issues that fuel the fire are related to who is going to be an insider. Those who have been moved to the outside will respond based on the changing nature of the relationship. This is predictable in every transition.

Here are some questions church members should be thinking about in the transition process:

1. What changes will occur in the pastor's inner circle as the new pastor's leadership team emerges? Who were the insiders under the leadership of the former pastor? Who has been left out of the new inner circle?
2. Analyze tension in the transition. Where is it coming from? Is the battle between tradition (old) and change (new)? Is the battle about power or position—or is it about different understandings of God's purpose?
3. What camps, if any, are battling within the congregation? Identify these camps and pray for discernment about what is fueling their actions. How will you talk with them? Hold them together? Love them and move them to where God wants them?
4. As a pastor, to whom are you listening? What information or emotions are you acting on? What are the ripple effects of your actions?
5. Who is feeling unheard, unattended to, or unloved? How are those feelings affecting their behaviors? Who is hurting and why? Who is pastoring these outsiders?
6. How can you love those who have been hardest hit by the transition? How might love serve as the foundation of reconciliation and healing in the transition?
7. What tangible acts of love are working to hold the congregation together and move them forward?

The questions are to be taken seriously and should be talked about openly. In transition, the tensions implicit in these questions are present in one form or another. When congregations, along with their pastor, are invited to have the conversations openly and name the joy and pain of transitions, the discussion helps to facilitate a process of moving the congregation forward.

As the new pastor comes in, both the church and the pastor have to be sensitive to what is going on. As the pastor builds his or her leadership team, the pastor must be mindful of who is invited to be on that team. Those who are on the new team have to be sensitive to those who are no longer a part of that inner circle. Pastors need a team of people who can be honest with them and help them lead in a such a way that it moves the congregation closer to what it is God wants them to become. Problems occur when the inner circle is used as power over others and as a way to isolate and ostracize parts of the congregation that aren't connected with that inner circle. Those who are part of the new leadership team have to be levelheaded, sensitive to the tension of old versus new, willing to reach out to all parts of congregation, and most of all they must represent the masses of the church and not just the upper class of power in the church.

The honest part of this conversation is that, in transitions, there will be tension and there will be fights. This is inevitable given our fallible humanity. The question is how will the church and pastor handle the fights? Spiritually discerning leaders hug the people we might prefer to punch. As Christians, we have to remember that our weapons are not carnal (2 Corinthians 10:3-4). The response in transitions must be rooted in love (1 Corinthians 13:4-7). This is a love that is patient because transitions take time. This is a love that is not proud or arrogant. It is not trying to have its way; rather, it is trying to find God's way. It is not a love that seeks to demolish those with whom it disagrees, but it is a love that seeks to be truthful and bound for reconciliation. In transition, the outreach of love in action has to be the order of the day.

The fights that are inevitable can't be seen as personal. The pastor has to take the high ground. The church is looking to the pastor as an example of how they are to deal with this tension. When the conversation in the church is reduced to gossiping about who is on what side and who has to be removed, when the pastor or new leadership team starts to "get people," the fight has degenerated into a frenzy that will not serve the church well. Pastors have to think about how the conversation can be elevated to a point where the church isn't talking about each other but rather they are talking about where God is leading them. There have to be times of prayer and discernment as the congregation seeks to rise above the mess and truly hear a message from God. This means that vision is a central part of what a pastor and church leadership team have to share with the larger congregation.

The church has to have a sense of where they are going. When the pastor and the leadership team share vision, the conversation moves from fights that are rooted in pain to hope that is rooted in the promise of God for the future of that church. In this conversation about vision, the past can't be neglected. A new vision for the future is in direct relationship to where the church has come from, its past. Churches should talk about the past with respect, even as they look forward to their future. This conversation is has to hold in sacred tension what was and what will be, while being sensitive to the pain of those who built what we now refer to as the past. Pastoral care and attention to all parts of the congregation must take precedence. The pain has to be managed in an environment of hope.

Reflection Questions

Congregation

1. How are we going to intentionally welcome our new pastor and his or her family over the first year?
2. How will we protect our new pastor's time so that he or she can learn our congregation and have time to focus on what is important?

3. Are we divided into camps? How can we come together for the good of our church?
4. How are we grieving what was and moving toward what we will become?
5. Where are we on our journey in becoming one with our new pastor? What are the things we need to deal with in order to move forward?

Pastor

1. How am I and my family going to love the people and accept their welcome?
2. How will I balance attention to family life, pastoral leadership, pastoral care, and community/denominational involvement?
3. What camps are active in the church?
4. How will I leave my old church behind?
5. Where are my family and I on our journey in becoming one with our new congregation? What are the things we need to deal with to move forward?

NOTES

1. Loren B. Mead, *A Change of Pastors . . . And How It Affects Change in the Congregation* (Herndon, VA: Alban Institute, 2005), 60.
2. Carolyn Weese and J. Russell Crabtree, *The Elephant in the Boardroom: Speaking the Unspoken about Pastoral Transitions* (San Francisco: Jossey-Bass, 2004), 48.
3. George B. Thompson Jr., *How to Get Along with Your Pastor: Creating Partnership for Doing Ministry* (Cleveland: Pilgrim Press, 2006), 66.
4. Mead, *A Change of Pastors*, 51.
5. Ibid., 53.
6. Ibid., 63.
7. Ibid., 63.
8. Ibid., 83.
9. Michael J. Coyner, *Making a Good Move: Opening the Door to a Successful Pastorate* (Nashville: Abingdon, 2000), 24.

|3|

The Forest
and the Trees

Pastoral Transitions in Two Perspectives

While multiple reasons and nuances surround every pastoral transition, this chapter looks at pastoral transitions from the macro level. In many cases, pastors and congregations caught in transitions can't see the forest for the trees. In transition, the trees are not to be demeaned or discounted, but the congregation and the new pastor have to keep the big picture in mind. The trees of transitions can be some of the unique circumstances of a transition in pastoral leadership—for example, when a church has a child following a parent, a widowed wife following her late husband, a young pastor following a much older pastor, or a postmodern upstart following a civil rights legend. And then what about the minister who follows a pastor who has been forced out in disgrace?

The various circumstances of transitions call for nuanced approaches to ushering each congregation into the new tenure of pastoral leadership. While I won't deal specifically with each type of transition, I do suggest that every congregation and potential new pastor think on the circumstances that precipitated the transition they are living in, and consider how they need to minister to that transition. At the same time, the cause of the transition doesn't change the overall season, culture, or leadership model of the church. These bigger-picture elements persist through transition, rather in the same way that a single tree falling in the woods leaves the vast acres of the forest largely unchanged but nonetheless affected. I in no way want to minimize the circumstances that surround each and every transition, because they do affect the transition process. As pastors and congregations make the transition, they must be cognizant of where the church is and where the congregation needs to go as they live in the moment of transition in relationship.

When a pastor takes a new church, and when a church calls a new pastor, many circumstances surround these transitions. I arrived at Ebenezer African Methodist Episcopal Church after Rev. William Estes suffered a fatal heart attack. This situation required me to be sensitive to his surviving family, who were still staying in the parsonage when I assumed the role as pastor. My wife, Vanessa, and I knew our first job was to minister to the grieving congregation, including the Estes family. As we journeyed with them during those first few months, we walked tenderly. My early preaching used a pastoral style that was centered on the grief process. As we came to the close of that period, we had a major worship service that included the Estes family and that encouraged the congregation to show the widow and family a lot of love.

As we went through that period, as much as we were ministering to this family, we were also trying to model for our congregation what Christian ministry looks like. The death of my predecessor made me more sensitive to the immediate vulnerability of the congregation, but I couldn't lose sight of the macro issues of the church's life cycle in which I was called to share leadership. Despite its current grief, this was a relatively stable congregation that didn't need much transformation, and it was this larger church situation that determined how I would lead in the initial phases of this new pastorate. Ebenezer had a strong music ministry and powerful worship experience, with a diverse population of both young and more mature African Americans. What was absent was a strong Bible study and an intentional focus on God's Word. My focus was twofold: I was assuming pastoral leadership of a congregation that had lost its pastor to an untimely and tragic death, while, at the same time, I was being called to lead a ministry in the process of realignment.

Realignment is one of the four motifs of an organization in transition, as identified by Dr. Michael Watkins, a reigning expert in the field of organizational transitions. I have found that the four organizational motifs he identifies in corporate settings are also relevant for congregational transitions. What he calls motifs might also be characterized as seasons in a church's life cycle. Those four seasons or motifs are start-up, turnaround, realignment, and sustaining success.[1]

Pastors, as you consider or accept leadership of a new church, you must identify the congregational motif or season of this church. Congregational leaders would be wise to ask a similar question: Where is our church on the continuum of start-up to sustaining success?

Start-up Congregations

In a start-up organization, the congregation and pastor must come together and build a foundation to resurrect a dead or near-dead church. My first pastoral assignment was to a closed church. Allen AME Church in Clearfield, Pennsylvania, was a start-up congregation when I arrived in 1991. All we had was a building, a few older members, and the name of one former member. I was instructed to find that former member and get the church reopened. Essentially, we had to start from scratch.

When a pastor is called to a transitional start-up, there is a sense of urgency. While the new pastor has to know the culture, history, and other pertinent information about the church, there is little time for learning and a huge need for doing. The congregation will have to give the new pastor license and support to bring the church back to life. Change is the order of the day. In the words of W. L. Bateman, "If you keep on doing what you've always done, you're going to keep on getting what you've always got." The situation demands triage; the new pastor is in a trauma situation.

Sometimes the difficulty with start-ups is that the members of the congregation may have become comfortable with their present state of being. When I was sent to Trinity AME Church in Pittsburgh, Pennsylvania, I walked into a church that reported five hundred members, but I only found twenty-five the week that I assumed the pastoral charge. The congregation was sitting in a building that held around three hundred fifty people, but the building was arid, cold, and old, and the balcony wasn't used for seating; it was a storage area. On our first Sunday at the church, my daughters cried because there were no children in the congregation.

One would think that the congregation would have been happy to have a young pastoral family come in and promise to lead in such a way as to bring new life to the church. The irony of the situation was that the congregation had arrived at their comfort level over years of decline. They knew each other, loved each other, and watched out for each other. They were the faithful few who had kept the doors open. They had a small community, and this tiny, faithful, loving community was comfortable.

When in the difficult season of a start-up transition, people can't be labeled demons because they resist the change that is needed. The pastor must love them into the change process while simultaneously respecting their love and the community they have formed over the years. As Trinity started to grow, we were taking in more members in my first year there than the church had received in the past fifteen years combined. This was massive change. The power brokers had been dethroned; people had been literally put out of their seats.

The leaders of the church wanted to go back to a day of high church, rich in AME liturgy. Instead, they had a young pastor who was rapping in the pulpit!

In a start-up transition, the new pastor must create a sense of urgency and will need to lead change that produces results quickly, gaining momentum and moving forward with love and respect for the people who asked and accepted him or her as their pastor. There is going to be resistance, but it must be handled biblically, delicately, and with sensitivity to the senior members. People have to be loved through their pain as the pastor and leadership make space for them to vent and share their concerns. Listen, even to disgruntled members, because there is something to be learned, and the members will feel heard. Listening means that the new pastor is willing to be moved. This isn't patronizing those who speak, but it is actively listening in love. Remember that the new pastor is pastor of *all* of the people, even those who don't want to follow where God is leading the church.

Start-ups require a healthy balance of doing while learning. To do a start-up right, the new pastor and the new leadership team have to take chances—in some cases big chances. At Trinity, I had to take the big chance of growing an inner-city church. I had to do this in the midst of leaders who had moved out of the community, were commuting to church, and didn't think much of our neighbors. The chance I took was to lead an evangelism plan that sought the folk next door. I was betting on a massive influx of people. I had to change the worship style, change the music, and adjust my preaching style to speak to the changing demographic of new church members who had previously been unchurched. These changes were painful but rewarding. In the end, I was going on a hunch from God, and God was in it. The church grew. Yes, there was resistance from some of our more senior members. The leading giver, a college professor, left the church, crying, "This church has become too ghetto." But I had to take a chance, and we survived.

The process of transitioning into a start-up has to include the development of a team of leaders who can support what they may not see. As the new pastor comes in, some of the old leaders may want to step down from their positions. There has to be a way for leaders to deselect and get off the team with little or no disgrace. A new leadership team will emerge that may be a hybrid, combining what was present when the new pastor arrived with emerging or new church leaders.

Leading change in start-ups is painful, and the new pastor must try to minimize the pain. The new team will have to support a vision that is radically different from what the congregation has been used to seeing. When I stood up at Trinity and said we were going to take in more than two hundred new members that year, the folk clapped while laughing. My leaders couldn't visualize what I was saying. I was asking them to support what they couldn't see. The majority of the people didn't support the vision because it appeared to be unrealistic and overly ambitious.

In both start-ups and turnarounds, in the midst of transitions, the pastor and leadership team have to minister to the doubt and unbelief. Don't condemn as traitors and workers from the devil those who fail to capture the vision. Put this transition in its sociological context. Church members may not have enough evidence or experience in that church to believe God is in what their new pastor is saying. Pastors, declare, "Thus says the Lord" anyway, and produce fruit! Use the honeymoon or grace period to implement changes that will make long-term and short-term differences.

Turnaround Congregations

In a turnaround congregation, the church isn't dead; it is sickly and wandering in the wrong direction. This church will need massive reorganization and a biblically centered focus if it hopes to survive. Many of our historic African American churches are turnarounds. They have a glorious past, but if they hope to thrive in the present age, they are going to have struggle with a new direction and new identity. The church leaders, with the new pastor, will have to define reality while participating in a process to envision a different future. That visioning process will help to determine where God wants to take the church.

This kind of turnaround transition can be very painful. The turnaround church typically has a stagnant or dwindling membership. Members may be in denial about the present while still celebrating the glory days of their past. They may want to recreate those glory days instead of dealing with current trends and present reality in order to build a new future.

In turnarounds, many of the challenges are similar to what we see in start-ups, yet there are key differences. In a turnaround, congregants haven't simply become comfortable; they may be in denial. They may not realize just how bad things are. After all, in turnarounds the church isn't dead yet. Membership hasn't fallen below twenty-five people, and there is still money in the endowment fund. True, memories of the glory years are growing dim, but the present seems stable enough to offer hope for the future.

That determination to cling to dim hope and deny the current reality puts many turnaround congregations in a disastrous decline. The turnaround church is bogged down in the past, and they may not realize they are stuck. Without intervention, the stagnant congregational life and practices will ensure the church's continued decline. In these types of transitions, resources have to be shifted, and the focus of the church has to be redirected to the areas that will make the church thrive.

The congregation has to be reenergized around the new focus of quality teaching, preaching, and Christian discipleship. People have to be convinced that change is necessary and have to be shown the potential benefits of these changes. In turnaround seasons, a church may not have to act as quickly as in a start-up, but the clock is ticking. Church leaders need to support and magnify the vision of the new pastor, so that the congregation is able to recognize the urgency of the need and join the efforts to implement God's plan for change.

A word of caution: Don't be surprised when the greatest hostility and resistance comes from those members who are most directly affected by the change. This is only natural because the growing pains of transition will be felt most profoundly by them.

Realignment Congregation

As was the case I encountered at Ebenezer, a church in need of realignment is one with significant strengths, but it also has serious challenges or constraints that are hindering its future success and clarity of direction. The pastor and church leaders will have to work to refocus the congregation and streamline the church's vision and ministry by choosing to do those things that bring the church more in line with where God wants to take them. A church in this situation may be blinded by the light of their strengths. That light shines so brightly, they might not be able see the dark spots. A realignment season presents a tricky transition because it calls on the new pastor and the current leadership to look beyond the obvious. There is no sense of urgency that gives support for the needed change. When a pastor and congregational leaders find themselves in this type of situation, it may be hard for them to convince the larger body of the need for change.

I am convinced that realignments are the trickiest to handle of the four transitional seasons. In realignments a pastor and the leadership team have to "challenge deeply ingrained cultural norms that no longer contribute to high performance."[2] In the first two types of transitions (start-ups and turnarounds), the focus is on acting for change. In the last two seasons (realignments and sustaining success), the focus is more on educating for change. The good news is that, in cases of realignment or sustaining success, both pastor and leadership have more time to learn because there isn't a sense of urgency. The challenge is that without a sense of urgency, it may take a while for the team to pass along its lessons learned to the congregation, whose members won't see a pressing need for change. In realignment seasons, the resistance often takes the form of "Why fix what ain't broke?"

The pastor and leadership will need to educate the members on the new vision from a biblical perspective. The changes will have to be implemented slowly and only after much study. The learning has to come before the doing. In the context of realignments, "it is important to understand the organization [church], get the strategy right, build support for it, and make some good calls early."[3] Early on, if wrong calls are made that don't show noticeable improvement in an already good situation, the pastor and those around the pastor will be attacked. In realignments, one must identify those things that will make the church markedly better. These changes can't be about a pastor's whims or wishes; they have to be about making the church a better biblical model with tangible signs of success that can be readily marked.

Realignments call for principled change of things that, if left unchanged, could derail the ministry and over time be the demise of the transition. When I went to Ebenezer, not implementing a strong Bible study for church leaders would have hampered the ministry over time. What would a church look like that had no biblical foundation? How can church leaders lead a biblically functioning church when there is no core teaching of the Bible in the church? Before implementing a Bible study, however, I had to learn about the church's history and understand why there wasn't a Bible study. When I came to the conclusion that we needed a Bible study, I had to convince the people why this was good for the church in the short term and long term. After implementing the Bible study, I had to show them how it was benefiting us all and the future of the church. In realignments, the new pastor has to study before making change; then the new pastor must sell the change and show how the change is adding to the life of the church.

Sustain-Success Congregations

A church in a sustaining-success season is one that is on the right track. The new pastor and congregation have to nurture the existing growth with minimal changes. This may mean that the new pastor doesn't have or need the latitude to make radical change. The only change in this type of congregation is simply to take them to the next level of excellence. When a pastor comes into a sustaining-success church and treats it like a start-up or turnaround, that pastor has a recipe for disaster.

The new pastor and leadership team may feel constrained in the sense that they might not be able to put their stamp on what is happening. Any needed changes are really a tweaking and not an overhaul. Pastors' egos have to take a back seat in sustaining success. Change can't be implemented because "I like it that way." The way the new pastor likes or had it at his or her previous church isn't what has to rule here. In a successful church, that church's existing priorities and vision have to inform how the new pastor leads. God has already shown how God wants to work in this situation at this church. The new pastor is obligated to honor how God has blessed this church.

Sustaining success gives the new leadership time to learn. There is no need to rush and do something. The new pastor and leadership team can be patient historians as they look back, see the connections in the present, and decide over time what it is going to take to get this ministry to the next level while also deciding what that next level will look like.

Two Roads Diverge in the Woods[4]

If the organizational motif that provides the big-picture backdrop for pastoral transitions is comparable to the life cycle of the forest, the church culture might be compared with the specific type of tree growing in that forest. The previous pastoral style is analogous to a particular tree that has fallen in that forest. We have already considered the seasons in a church life cycle. Let us shift now to consider the church culture.

Any church at any time in its history may find itself facing any of the four organizational motifs for transition. In contrast, a church culture will develop more organically, often in direct relationship to the style of leadership established by a founding or otherwise influential pastor. Each pastor brings a highly personal style to the ministry, and the relationship that develops between leader and congregation is typically based on that style. Therefore, a change in pastoral leadership may introduce a culture clash between new pastor and the existing congregation—especially if the search committee or denominational judicatory determines that the church would benefit from a change in leadership style.

A faith community will formulate expectations about the new pastor through the lens of what they saw in their previous pastor. In successful transitions, everyone involved understands who is leaving and who is coming and what the congregation's expectations are in terms of pastoral leadership.

Church leaders must be aware of the tension created with the arrival of a new pastor whose approach to ministry and relationships is diametrically different from the previous pastor. Pastors, when moving into a new situation, must be clear on what the folk expect based on the kind of leadership model the predecessor established.

Four different leadership models describe the vast majority of congregational cultures: family culture, icon culture, archival culture, and replication culture.[5] Note that these models characterize the expected relationship between pastor and congregation. Just as every church is positioned in a particular organizational motif, so each church also presents with a preexisting pastor-church culture that must be taken into consideration. This cultural component is vital to understanding the transitional issues facing a newly arrived pastor.

Awareness of this component is heightened in the African American church, where the pastor is typically the central wheel around which the pastor-church relationship revolves.

Family Culture

In this church culture, the relationship between pastor and congregation is an intimate one. The pastor is viewed as a parent, guardian, or elder sibling who has accepted responsibility for protecting and nurturing the church family. In this pastor-congregation relationship, people expect to have access to the pastor. Members will expect the pastor to be present on Sunday mornings and available throughout the week to individuals and to groups. They expect their pastor to marry, bury, visit, and counsel them in every stage of life. While this culture may develop in both small and large churches, for obvious reasons, it is more challenging to sustain in larger congregations where the pastor-member ratio is quite daunting. Such a highly relational culture will not tolerate an aloof or inaccessible pastor.

The family culture breeds closeness and is a loving atmosphere. However, with this being the case, it is also the most difficult culture for a new pastor to become the true pastor. Because the congregation is so close to the former pastor, loving the new pastor can be seen as betrayal. The relationship that the congregation had with the former pastor lingers even in that person's absence, so it is difficult for the congregation and the new pastor to form a bond.

On the other hand, the way in which this congregation will form a bond with the new pastor is in the context of intense relationship building. The way to deal with a family culture is simple: be around the family, sit with the family, eat with the family, talk with the family, and let the family adopt you. As the new pastor is present and active in the lives of the members, he or she begins to be seen as part of the family. The new pastor has to open up to the family, allow the family to show their love. Let them extend acts of kindness, and return those acts with love. The culture of the family church will eventually embrace their new pastor and new relationship.

Icon Culture

In an iconic culture, the pastor is the embodiment and ambassador of the church. The relationship between pastor and congregation in this culture is synonymous with the church itself. The pastor is the church. When congregants are out in the community, they don't say they are members of Solid Rock Baptist Church; they declare they are members of Rev. Dr. Smith's church—and they fully expect their pastor's name to be recognized in the community, the region, and even the nation or the world. The iconic pastor is a larger-than-life leader whom the church elevates and takes pride in being associated with. The congregation expects their pastor to be a model of what the church stands for—always out front, appearing at the right events and saying the right things, always involved with the right causes or committees, always sought after by other leaders and by the media. The pastor in this culture is expected to be a public figure. Celebrity is valued over accessibility.

When a new pastor arrives at the icon-culture church, the issue becomes filling the shoes of the icon. The ghost of the icon is bigger than life. On the one hand, the new pastor inherits a certain status as he or she follows the icon. This status will give the new pastor clout in the community, but it can also constrain him or her as the new pastor tries to redefine how to wear these shoes he or she has been called to fill. When a new pastor follows an icon, he or she also has clout with the church members as they are looking for the new pastor to represent them. A new pastor can use this clout as leverage to learn and re-image what this new icon will look like. A pastor can also be led, of course, to attempt to transform the culture of any church, but he or she must first understand where the church is and must define the new direction. This is most difficult in the icon culture, because the icon is sometimes like an idol. People's idols have to be dismantled, not blown up. If a pastor decides to radically alter the icon culture, he or she must be intentional and patient. Icons don't go away easily.

Archival Culture

The pastor in an archival-church culture is a keeper of the past. The key pastoral relationship in this culture is not with current members but with the legacy of previous generations. The congregation expects their leader to hold the line, protect the tradition, and honor the old ship of Zion. The pastor must know the tradition of the church, must be active in the larger denomination, must sing the old hymns, must wear the right religious garb, and must be a keeper of the Lord's house. The congregation won't expect or appreciate their pastor's service outside the church walls. Individuals are less important than the community, and the present and future tend to be valued only to the extent that the traditions of the past are preserved and enshrined in days to come. The church expects its pastor to be proud of these traditions and to nurture them for the next generation.

There is a rich heritage and respect for history in the archival culture. The respect for tradition means that these churches understand and know their history as an African American church. They realize that it was their history that "brought them safe thus far."[6] The archival culture, while being rich in history, can also be held hostage by its history. It can have a tendency to fight modernization and change. The past becomes something to be worshipped, and the pastor is to represent that past. The new pastor may be resisted simply because he or she is young or reaches out to youth and young-adult culture. The push back in archival culture is a push to go back, stay back, and lay back.

Replication Culture

In a replication culture, the replication in question is equipping the saints to follow (i.e., imitate and replicate) Christ's example as disciples. The relationship between pastor and congregation is that of teacher and student. As leader, the pastor empowers the church to serve through traditional roles of biblical teaching and preaching. While the pastor is expected to be the public face of the ministry as teacher and preacher, he or she may have license to delegate many pastoral-care responsibilities such as visitation, counseling, and officiating weddings and funerals. As keeper and sharer of knowledge, the pastor is expected to spend the majority of his or her time in study, preparing for major teaching moments and leading the church from behind the scenes. The replication-culture church values education and preparation over accessibility or celebrity. The church is comfortable with the daily ministry of the church being carried out by associate ministers and lay leaders.

The replication culture appreciates good preaching and teaching. Their high standards for preaching and teaching afford the pastor the time prepare a word. On the other hand, when a new pastor enters a congregation with these types of demands, it may be difficult to carve out the time for preparation in the midst of the demands of a new pastoral relationship. There is struggle for the pastor's time of building relationships on the one hand and preparing to preach and teach on the other hand. This balance can be tricky.

Understanding and Articulating Expectations

One of the key cultural components that have to be taken into consideration during transitions is the relationship that existed between the congregation and previous pastor, because that sets up expectations for the new pastor. During transitions, churches have to be cognizant of what type of relationship they had with the former pastor and what type of relationship they expect with the new pastor. If a new pastor is more of a replication-culture pastor who wants time to prepare sermons and Bible studies and who takes great pride in this part of the calling, and he or she is following a pastor who was deeply rooted and promoted a family culture, the new pastor and the church are going to have problems. The congregation will feel slighted by what they see as the pastor not paying attention to them or not loving them, while the pastor is saying, "I am loving you by preaching and teaching." This tension amplifies why it is so important for churches and pastors to be aligned before the call or appointment. If they find out after the fact that these differences exist, they have to decide how they are going to work through them.

The dynamic of time in these situations must also be considered. Building relationships takes time—a fact that is especially significant internally for family-culture churches and externally for iconic churches. Congregations will have to acknowledge their expectations openly, and then be encouraged to approach the new relationship with patience and commitment. When expectations from the past are projected onto the present, all parties need to talk openly and negotiate graciously. Sometimes pastors don't understand why the folk aren't pleased and vice versa; in many cases, they have not sat back and analyzed the demands in a transition that is based on pastor-congregation relationship expectations.

Reflection Questions

Church leaders

- What type of pastoral relationship did we experience with our previous pastor?
- How satisfied were our members with that relational culture? Why?

- Does our congregation expect continuity in their relationship with the new pastor, or would they prefer a different kind of relationship—and why?

Pastor

- What kind of relationships have you experienced between pastor and congregation—as a pastor, as a congregant, and as a church leader?
- What type of relationship are you most comfortable in cultivating as a leader?
- What kind of relationship did your new congregation have with your predecessor?
- How will you approach that church culture—with a commitment to maintaining it or with a strategy for changing it?

Leading with Style in the Midst of Conflict

The last big-picture issues to be considered in transitions are the personality and style of the religious leader who is leaving—and of the leader who is coming or who is yet to come. In his book *Black Religious Leaders: Conflict in Unity*, author Peter Paris outlines four major pastoral types of leaders in the African American church. These types ought to be used in evaluating the styles and personalities of the outgoing pastor and of the incoming candidates. Different church cultures need different kinds of pastors, and these four leadership profiles should be helpful in assessing past leaders and desirable future leadership. Remember, past experience creates expectations—both on the part of the congregation (based on the previous pastor) and on the part of the incoming pastor (who has experienced various styles of leadership).

Paris identifies four religious leadership styles: priestly type, prophetic type, political type, and nationalist type. Too often, especially in pastoral transitions shadowed by scandal or tainted by conflict, churches will choose a pastor whose leadership style is the polar opposite of their previous leader. Such decisions are usually motivated by a misunderstanding of the church's organizational motif. The congregation may assume it needs a turnaround transition, when in reality, only a realignment is necessary. When the new pastor arrives with a dramatically different style and an assumption that dramatic change is also needed, conflict is the inevitable result. Church leaders and potential pastors need to assess the former pastor's style of leadership alongside the overall church culture and organizational motif. Note the distinct differences and emphases between just the first two leadership models: the priestly type and the prophetic type.

The Priestly Type

The priestly-style pastor has an internal focus and bent. He or she is very comfortable serving inside the four walls of the church and tends to see this focus as essential to pastoral ministry. Paris defines the priestly pastoral style this way:

> The role and function of priests is to serve the temple (that is, the house of God). Their ministry is to represent God to the people and to intercede on behalf of the people before God, and/or to instruct the people firmly and authoritatively about the nature of their religious responsibilities and obligations. . . . The priest aims at no significant societal change. Rather, the basic structures of the society are perceived as fundamentally good and worthy of God's favor, being sought through prayer and supplication. In brief, the societal structures are thought to be grounded in the ideals of God and, for the most part, are viewed as already actualized."[7]

The priestly style pastor will have an internal focus. If a priest-type leader is appointed to a congregation that has had pastors who were community organizers or if the church is very active in the community, there are going to be style and expectation conflicts between that pastor and the congregation. An incoming pastor needs to put his or her leading pastoral style on the table and be honest with a congregation up front. When a priestly style pastor is following a priestly style pastor, he or she will need time to develop that intimate bond with the congregation as he or she cares for them, teaches them, and takes care of the temple. Even when there are similar styles from the previous pastor to the new pastor, there still has to be flexibility as to how the new pastor lives out his or her call at this time in the life of the congregation. The new pastor must be seen on his or her own terms and not through lens of the former pastor.

The Prophetic Type

The second style Paris identifies in his work is the prophet. The prophet has been one of the most outspoken types of pastors we have seen in the African American tradition.

> Prophets are reformers. They never accommodate the status quo and often are viewed as social misfits. They tend to make people uncomfortable, even the ones with whom they are closely associated . . . prophets are purists in terms of both theological doctrine and political principle. They flatly reject any compromise relative to either. They are oriented to an ideal past and see vividly the estrangement of present thought and practice from their roots. They boldly expose that estrangement in courageous forms of action and in speech that is both shocking and perceptive. The prophets view God as the source of social justice and are absolutely certain that God is on their side in the quest for social reform."[8]

The prophet pastor is the stereotypical civil rights–era pastor. Examples of this archetype who come to mind are Rev. Dr. Hosea Williams and Rev. Dr. J. Alfred Smith Sr. The best of the African American tradition has been epitomized in our prophetic preachers. In many parts of the country, this type of pastor is hard to find today. This is unfortunate considering the state of the average African American: still fighting to climb the ladder of success; filling the jails; being sent to overcrowded, underfunded public schools; falling victim to inner-city poverty. Churches and potential new pastors would do well to consider the relevance and value of the prophetic leadership style.[9]

The prophetic pastor is a close cousin to the next leadership style, the political pastor. The nuances that differentiate them, however, are significant when looking at past and future pastors and evaluating what a congregation will tolerate and support.

The Political Type

The political leader is outspoken like the prophet; yet, his or her focus tends to be on compromise. They are not seen as social misfits or troublemakers. They tend to appear to the media as more logical and rational. The prophet is seen as pushing too fast or too hard, wanting change now. Many of the conservatives in the white and black communities considered the civil rights leadership to be prophets; the likes of Rev. Dr. Martin L. King Jr. and Rev. Fred Shuttlesworth were seen in the prophetic role. The distinction between prophet and political style can be significant when looking at who has led and who will lead a congregation. Paris defines the political-type pastor:

> The political type of religious leadership is closely related to the prophetic type, the chief difference being its tendency to focus less on the relationship between politics and religion and more on problem-solving techniques. The political type readily assumes a theological grounding of politics but is not inclined toward giving theological justification for every political thought or act. In other

words, although it admits a positive relationship between religion and politics, it does not confuse the two and never attempts to reduce the one to the other.[10]

For me, Pastor Chip Murray at First AME Los Angeles represents the epitome of the political leadership style. He saw the value in engaging the larger society in his fight for change. Pastors who are political types use the church as leverage to make a difference in the larger society. While they can be great hands-on pastors, they are called to a larger field of ministry that sends them to city hall and the state house. Churches that want or call this type of leader have to be willing to share their pastor with the city and community. This is inward leadership style with an outward focus. The pastor focuses on preaching a word in the church that leads to action outside the church.

When Pastor Murray retired from First AME, the bishop appointed a pastor who was more priestly in style (with an internal focus on taking care of the temple). As a result, the tension in the congregation and community was exacerbated. Pastor John, who followed Pastor Chip, wasn't a political type. He had an appreciation for the prophetic and political styles of pastors, but he was secure and comfortable in his priestly style. The bishop may have been trying to shift the focus of the congregation by sending a different style of pastor to First AME. That's fine, but the congregation and the new leadership have to own up to and deal with these different style and expectations. In essence, when this type of diametric difference in leadership style follows the other, what it means to be pastor of the congregation has to be redefined publicly and privately, with the congregation and the church leadership.

In yet another contrast, while the political religious leader engages the system and agitates for change, the nationalist leader wants to overhaul the system and is seeking radical, revolutionary change.

The Nationalist Type

While prophets speak truth to power, priests pray for those in power, and political types work with those in power, the nationalist is comfortable to sit outside the system and create an entirely new world for his or her people. Nationalist-type pastors are comfortable with those who would lead a church like The Shrine of the Black Madonna in Atlanta. They are what I like to call *oppositional leaders*, stewards of new and radical knowledge that leads to positive revolutionary thinking and acting. Paris defines the type this way:

> The nationalist type of leadership aims at a fundamental reordering of the structures and values of the society. Its goal is a new social order with little or no continuity with the old. Consequently, it appeals to no historical precedents apart from references to similar imperatives for radical social change in other times and places. Unlike the prophetic style, this type is convinced that the society lacks the capacity for repentance since it is viewed as morally decadent to the core.[11]

For churches that are comfortable being on the outside fighting, this is the type of leader they would want. A nationalist pastor is like Malcolm X or Albert Cleage. These were both African American religious leaders who didn't have faith in America or in what they saw as the racist social system. They condemned the system and sought a reordering of society. The nationalist leader's audience is his or her people. They aren't as concerned with convincing the system to help their people. They want to convince the people to help themselves. Their ministry is focused on the hearts and minds of their people. They speak to their people, teach them, share their revolutionary thinking with them, and act on this thinking in their world. They build their own community, businesses, and schools for the purpose of liberating their people from the chains of white supremacy. The nationalist is building a black nation within the nation.

Reflection Questions

Church Leaders

- What type of leader do we need?
- What type of leader do we want? (Sometimes what we need and what we want are different things.)
- What type of leader have we had in the past?
- What are the leadership styles of the candidates whom we are now considering?

Pastors

- What type of leader are you?
- What type of leader preceded you in this congregation?
- What type of leader do you think this congregation wants (or needs)?
- What type of leader might you become through this transition?

These questions are critically important, whether a congregation is selecting a new leader through a search committee or the denomination is assigning the new pastor through its own discernment process. As church leaders and pastors, we may not have the luxury of choosing one another, but for the sake of the ministry, these questions can be valuable tools in learning to work together for the good of God's people.

Leading in Style and Time

As we have seen, the three big-picture issues in pastoral transitions are closely intertwined. They are rendered even more complex when we recognize that each one—the congregational motif, the pastor-church relationship culture, and the religious leadership style—must also be considered over time. In the past tense, where has the church been? What kind of relationship did they have with their previous pastor? What type of leadership style are they accustomed to? In the present tense, where is the church now? What kind of relationship and leadership style are they communicating a desire or need for today? And moving into the future, where is the church going? What kind of leader and pastor-congregation relationship will best serve God's purpose in getting them to that goal?

When everyone involved has clarity on the major transitional variables, that mutual understanding facilitates a healthier transition. Talk about these issues with the denominational judicatory, among the church leadership team, and in the initial interview with the pastoral candidates. Continue to talk about the issues as they evolve during the first year of the transition, including the congregation as much as possible in the conversations. These variables and expectations cannot be allowed to sit as elephants in the room. They are the driving forces of success or failure in transitions.

Reflection Questions

For Churches

1. What congregational motif describes our church: start-up, turnaround, realignment, or sustain success?
2. What was the nature of our previous pastor-congregation relationship? What are the expectations for our new pastor?
3. What type of leadership style is required for the change we need?

For Pastors

1. What type of congregational transition do I want to lead: start-up, turnaround, realignment, or sustain success?
2. What kind of church culture am I most comfortable with? What kind of relationship do I want with the congregation?

3. What would it take for me to become the leader this
congregation needs? Am I willing to do what is needed?
Why or why not?

NOTES

1. Michael Watkins, *Critical Success Strategies for New Leaders at All Levels: The First 90 Days* (Boston: Harvard Business School Press, 2003), 61–62.

2. Ibid., 66.

3. Ibid., 68.

4. Robert Frost, "The Road Not Taken," *Mountain Interval* (New York: Henry Holt and Company, 1916).

5. Carolyn Weese and J. Russell Crabtree, *The Elephant in the Boardroom: Speaking the Unspoken about Pastoral Transitions* (San Francisco: Jossey-Bass, 2004), 62.

6. John Newton, "Amazing Grace," 1779.

7. Peter Paris, *Black Religious Leaders: Conflict in Unity* (Louisville: Westminster/John Knox, 1991), 17–18.

8. Ibid., 20.

9. Marvin McMickle, *Where Have All the Prophets Gone?* (Cleveland: The Pilgrim Press, 2006).

10. Paris, *Black Religious Leaders*, 21.

11. Ibid., 22.

|4|

Taken by Surprise

Rev. Brenda Gregg and
Allen Chapel AME Church

Allen Chapel African Methodist Episcopal Church in Pittsburgh, Pennsylvania, was founded in 1869 as a mission
church on the Northside of Pittsburgh. The first pastor, Rev.
W. Riley, was appointed in 1881 and served until 1888. This
historic church had been pastored by the likes of the legendary Rev. Reverdy Ransom, who became one of the great bishops of the church. Fast-forward to October 1978, when Rev.
David U. Brown was assigned to be the pastor of the historic
Allen Chapel AME Church. Rev. Brown was a hands-on manager who was very involved in the community. Allen Chapel
had grown to be player in Pittsburgh politics, a tradition that
reached back to the days of Reverdy Ransom. Pastor Brown
would serve Allen Chapel as its pastor until 1992. This historic congregation was the epitome of an archival church.

Prior to Rev. Brown's coming, and over the fourteen years
of his service, the once-full church had dwindled with the
exodus from the city of Pittsburgh. By the time he left the
church, a faithful few were still holding on. A political-type

pastor, Rev. Brown was rooted in the community and very active in the local ministerial alliance. His participation as a civic leader was significant and made an impact in the larger community. As the new bishop came to Pittsburgh, changes were bound to be made. The new bishop, Henry Allen Belin, would take the bold step of appointing to Allen Chapel its first female pastor. In doing so, he made the decision to treat an apparently dying church as a start-up congregation.

A Time for Everything

Rev. Brenda Gregg would be that new pastor, assigned to Allen Chapel AME Church in 1992. When asked how she knew it was time to leave Bethel AME Church in Monroeville, Pennsylvania, she said, "I was dry. I was struggling to find a fresh word for the people. I was struggling in Bible study; I was struggling on Sunday morning. I had taken them as far as I could, and it was time to move." She had only been at Bethel AME for two years. There was no war going on between her and the members, but she knew she was done.

Pastors who are attuned to God's voice know when their seasons are up; they have a sense that it is time to go. It isn't about the people and how they feel, but it is about how God is ministering to that pastor to make the next move. Pastors have to be honest with themselves and recognize when they have taken a church where God wants them to take it, knowing it is time to move and letting the next pastor finish the job. Congregations also need to be able to assess where the leader is on the journey. I am not encouraging members to put pastors out, but congregations, like pastors, need be sensitive to that point in the ministry when it is time for a change. When is there a struggle? When is the work done? What Rev. Gregg felt at Bethel was her sign. When pastors and congregations have the sense that seasons have come to an end, they must have conversations that facilitate transition.

Upon her assignment to Allen Chapel, Rev. Gregg, like many starting pastors in the AME church, was happy to be moved. She was at the front end of her ministerial career, and the move meant a promotion. Rev. Gregg remarked, "It was the first church I had pastored where the steps went up instead of down."

Rev. Gregg was assigned to Allen at the annual conference, which closed on a Saturday. She scurried back to her now former church that evening to make arrangements for her replacement. She had been preparing for this day and had gone the extra mile before the annual conference to collect all the major documents, papers, and reports and neatly organize them for her successor. She removed her robes and all her other personal items from the office. As members saw her care, a few stopped in to offer their good wishes. She wrote a note for the incoming pastor, welcoming her and leaving contact information. Placing her keys on the desk, she said goodbye. She was on to Allen Chapel.

A Shock for Everyone

The next day was Sunday. Rev. Gregg got up early, prepared her family, and off to the church they went. She arrived prior to what she thought was the Sunday-school hour, pulled up to the church, and saw no one. She, along with her family, sat patiently in the car. She noticed an elderly woman crossing the street and moving toward the church. The lady scurried up to the door and opened it. Rev. Gregg, along with her family, waited until the lady was securely in and then they proceeded into the church. They exchanged pleasantries, and the woman told Rev. Gregg that the pastor wasn't going to be there today. Rev. Gregg responded, "I am your new pastor. Bishop appointed me yesterday." With a look of shock on her face, the woman responded in a loud voice, "Where is Rev. Brown?" This was the welcoming committee for Rev. Gregg: one woman, shocked and dismayed about this new pastor. Rev. Brown had not prepared this congregation for transition. After all, he had been reappointed to his church for the past sixteen years; he was completely unprepared to be moved. He wasn't expecting the change and was shocked at the annual conference when he wasn't reassigned. Consequently, he didn't make any overtures of congratulation or connection to Rev. Gregg. It was as if his church had been taken from him.

On that first Sunday of the new era of leadership, the new pastor was treated like an interloper. Rev. Gregg proceeded into her new church and sat and waited as other members made their way in. The attendance was a normal one for Allen AME: a sanctuary that sat three hundred was filled with empty seats, as twenty or so active members showed up. No children, no young adults, but the faithful, more mature saints who, along with Rev. Brown, had kept the doors open as Allen continued to play that role of being a symbolic reservoir for the political conversations and elite of Pittsburgh. After worship, the members tried to be nice to their new pastor, and she eventually got a key by the end of the day.

When Rev. Gregg got into her new office, she didn't find a note of welcome or a set of keys, and she didn't find a binder of organized documents. She found a mess. In the tiny cubicle of an office, unopened mail was stacked literally from the floor to the ceiling. She sat in that little office wondering if this was a promotion or a demotion.

She had been sent to lead this band of believers back to life. Ironically, Rev. Gregg had preached a one-night revival at Allen for the last two years. She knew the church had declined in membership. A bright note on her first Sunday was that, in that core of those who had remained at Allen, there were a few who had been a part of the committee that had invited her as a guest preacher. She was grateful to remember one in particular: Dr. Cotton had been that member standing up in the church and reflecting on how she had heard Rev. Gregg preach at the one-night revivals.

Managing the Dark Side:
Obstacles to Overcome

The church's lack of preparation for the transition was not Rev. Gregg's only obstacle. She was a female bivocational pastor who was also a single parent and a hospital administrator, transitioning into a church and a community that had been led by male pastors. The gender barriers were up and active. She was also trying to develop relationships with her fellow clergy in the community who had strong ties to Rev. Brown, ties that had been developed over sixteen years. Rev. Gregg needed to manage the dark side: shades of sexism and a general resistance to change. The hurdles she was facing seemed insurmountable, but the race was on, and she saw this as a marathon and not a sprint.

Rev. Gregg wisely decided to proceed slowly and gently. She didn't construct an atmosphere of winners and losers; rather, she knew right away that she had to be a team player and keep folk on the team who were already in the game. There was no manual for her to follow. As she tried to navigate this journey without a compass or a map, she decided to honor the tradition she had been given.

Not only was the church not prepared, but Rev. Gregg also knew that she had a steep learning curve. She had inherited a small congregation; her intent was not to alienate but to assimilate. She had to become one of them, and she was honoring that process by getting to know them through their rituals, their traditions, and their history. She didn't try to change them overtly; however, her very presence, preaching, and teaching were changing them. Her presence was making a difference, so as she was being assimilated, she was also socializing them into what they would become together. Rev. Gregg said, "I decided I didn't want to lose the people that I had. I didn't want to hurt them; I wanted to love them. I wanted to be their pastor. This was my goal, to become their pastor. I knew that an appointment didn't make me their pastor; it only gave me an opportunity to become their pastor." She understood that she had to be assimilated into the life of the community and the congregation, to the people, their ways and tradition. She couldn't know their ways or traditions without learning. She also didn't panic because the church was so small; she took her time and was patient as she transitioned into becoming their pastor. Rev. Gregg understood that pastors and congregations that make transitions well know this is for the long haul.

Because she didn't know the traditions of the church and the relationships with the larger community, she had to learn where to show up and then honor those traditions. All of the traditions the church had historically celebrated she blessed, celebrated, and participated in. In the ecumenical services, she blessed traditions within the church and with other churches. Rev. Gregg was honoring the past and, in so doing, she was leading the church in the work of grieving and processing a transition that they weren't prepared for.

Being Faithful with a Few

It was clear to Rev. Gregg that Rev. Brown had a core of committed members who were dedicated to that church and that community. While the small band of believers could have been looked at negatively, Rev. Gregg chose to see and focus on the good. Every pastor who follows another pastor has to seek the healthy parts of the church that the predecessor has left for him or her to build on. Rev. Gregg didn't despise this foundation but saw it as the springboard to build a vibrant growing congregation. She had a certain level of respect for her predecessor and for the leadership that she found when she arrived at the church. Rev. Gregg understood that tearing up the foundation that was laid would lead to chaos and disaster.

"I didn't take any of them out of office," she explained. Every officer who was leading when she inherited Allen Chapel remained in place. They were respected for what they had done and what they could add to the life of the church. By choosing to grow leaders and allow them to continue to be a part of the future of the church, Rev. Gregg empowered them to be agents for change.

When leaders choose to work with what they find, it calls for hard work. The new pastor has to build authentic relationships with the leaders, training and empowering them to lead. The leaders have to know the pastor's heart and vision for the church. This knowledge and mutual trust can only be built over time.

Taking a Team Approach to Transition

Rev. Gregg's strategy was to team the senior members with the new members who were coming into the church. There wasn't a line of demarcation between the old and the new. As the new sat beside the old, there was an integration and expansion of ministry, and a new vision emerged. For example, Rev. Gregg partnered a new member with the superintendent of Sunday school, expanding, not disbanding, the Christian education ministry of the church.

In the midst of all the attempts to expand, we can't forget the "welcoming committee" who asked, "Where is Rev. Brown?" The fact is that the church wasn't prepared for transition. Now they had a female pastor, and because they had never been pastored by a woman, there were gender issues on top of the traumatic transition. There is always some animosity and pain in a new pastoral relationship. The more complex the transition, the greater the pain—on all sides. The new pastor must be careful not to take his or her pain and frustration out on the congregation; they are hurting too. There has to be a place in the pastor's life where one feels affirmed and loved so that he or she will not lash out at the congregation.

Rev. Gregg had a church secretary and a few family members in the congregation who supported and loved her in such a way that she was enabled to love the congregation through the transition and preach sermons that would grow them and not club them. In transitions, pastors have to be careful not to beat the sheep. When pastors take the pain of transition so personally that they are incapable of loving and caring for the sheep, the question becomes, who is pastoring the people? Pastors have to ask themselves: am I feeding them or beating them? Am I directing them or driving them? Am I loving them or despising them? Am I big enough to overlook the past and see the future? Am I taking it personally?

As the team was being built, despite tensions, Rev. Gregg began to articulate the vision—and to push forward with a visible change process. The pastor has to decide what action or actions the congregation can withstand that will nudge them but not destroy them—what signs will move them forward. The pastor has to find out what is doable that will challenge and open the eyes of the congregation to begin to see the future.

From Vision to Decision

The renovation of the sanctuary was that stimulus for Rev. Gregg. The church was darkly paneled and had no carpet, only wooden floors. The church was so dark that it felt like night in the church in the middle of the day. Rev. Gregg stepped out—after having conversations with the members—and she made the decision to renovate the church. During the renovation, they worshipped in the church basement. This was early in her administration, within the first year; so, this was the big change that she was willing to spend her grace chips on. As the congregation saw the renovation, they owned this new look. And along with the new look came new members. The church began to grow. When leaders and their leadership team decide to make an investment or move forward in the midst of the transition, they have to be wise. The congregation and the community are watching. If the decision to act on a major initiative is successful, it can add life to the transition; if it fails it can stall the transition process.

Rev. Gregg had established the take off of an upward trajectory by being inclusive of the old, integrating the new, and choosing the right spark to move the church forward. There has to be support for this act or acts that nudge the church forward. However, the new pastor must expect some opposition. The decision to change will not be unanimous, and this action will cost the new pastor some support and will result in some members being so angered that they will either leave the church or take sides against the pastor and the change process. Pastors and members who support the change can't take it personally, though—it isn't personal, resistance to change is present in every organization.

As the transition moves forward, the pastor has to work at making sure that the change and the positive results of the change aren't about them but it are about the growth of the church. The larger congregation has to own the change and be invited to celebrate its positive results. To put it another way, they have to get some of the credit for what has happened. In the end this isn't about the pastor; it is about what God is doing with this church.

As the change benefits became apparent, the resistance to the change dissipated. Rev. Gregg found that the members were proud of how their church looked. They were proud of the growth in membership. Their pride translated into trusting the leadership of their new pastor. By building on the strength of the archival church's history and standing in the community, she was making right decisions that resulted in their being a better church. They were so proud of their new pastor and their newly renovated church that they wanted to have even more community meetings at their facility. They extended invitations to the city leaders to come to Allen. Moreover, they started to open up and share more with their new pastor about how she could become integrated into the life of the community. And in those community events, they made sure she was on the program representing Allen Chapel. As she made sure she was representing them and not herself, they beamed with pride, as they were becoming pastor and congregation, one Allen AME Church.

Turning Points in Transition

The congregation began to see the possibilities for Allen. They were moving from past to present and willing to consider the future. There is always a turning point in the life of a pastorate that the pastor needs to be aware of and make sure the members see as well. It is that point where they begin to lean forward. The new pastor truly becomes the pastor, and the majority of members begin to see the vision God has given via the pastor. They begin to see the vision, believe the vision, and work to make the vision come to fruition.

When Allen had thrived through the renovation, it began the push to see what God had for the future of their church. Rev. Gregg knew she was at that magical moment, and she and the church had seized this opportunity. Rev. Gregg exposed them to successful models of ministry around the country. They literally traveled as a team to see what they could be. As they traveled, the expansion of the Christian education ministry empowered them—from Bible study to workshops on every topic imaginable. These workshops weren't a loose hodgepodge of activity, but they were structured in such a way as to grow mature Christians leaders in the church. Mature Christian leaders respect, know, and live according to God's Word, hearing God's voice and supporting what God is doing in their church. Pastors have to empower the congregation to literally see what is possible.

Rev. Gregg said, "Every year I would determine what would be our learning curve for this year. I would tie that learning curve to the theme for the year, and we would focus on it.

For example, it may be youth ministry this year. I would have a theme around youth for the year and have classes taught all year around that theme. Every year we did a theme and I would then ask, what is it we don't know about that? You say you are expecting them to change, but unless you are giving them the tools they can't."

As the church began to change, those who wouldn't come to the training and weren't willing to grow were disassociated from leadership. Allen was a church that respected commitment to the life of the church as demonstrated through service. When service had been extended to include being extensively trained, the old timers and the newcomers penalized those who weren't willing to put in the time. Those who weren't willing to put the time in were sidelined by the membership. Rev. Gregg understood that Rev. Brown had built this amazingly loyal community of workers who were dedicated to their church. She extended this and used the commitment barometer to make the church stronger. She was developing organizational alignment. The church was lining up with the vision by being empowered to know, understand, and support the vision with the tools necessary to move forward.

When asked what were the keys to her successful transition, Rev Gregg said, "Be open-minded; you don't have all of the gifts. You have to want the gifts to come into the ministry." It is important for the pastor to seek to expand the gift set of the ministry by being inclusive and not exclusive. "Be willing to see things differently." The new pastor comes in with a set of eyes and expectations and has to expand his or her view and be willing to be changed in the change process as well.

In the midst of change, Rev. Gregg advises, the new leader must "be willing to hold on to the sacred important history. Be willing hold on to the traditions of the faith." What a pastor inherits has value and must be respected. The traditions in the church have held the community together. They deserve to be respected, and this respect for tradition will—in turn—earn the pastor a certain respect from the members.

"[Be] willing to combine the old with the new," Rev. Gregg says. "You have to pair the old guard with the new guard. If you can, allow the old and new to become equal partners, let the old shepherd the new. In this relationship they learn to respect each other and become each other's advocates."

Times of transition are about integration and transformation. "Everybody has to have a voice. Everybody has to feel like they are being heard." After all, "We are a family. We fuss like a family. We are dysfunctional like a family. But we are a family." Rev. Gregg was committed to growing a family and keeping the family together. The family has expanded, bought a new building, and moved across the community, but through it all, Allen AME is still "a family church purposed to obedience."

|5|

Being Led by the Spirit

Bishop Noel Jones and
Greater Bethany Community Church

Bishop Robert Wilson McMurray served as pastor of Greater Bethany Apostolic Church from 1962 until his transition to glory on May 28, 1994. (For those like me who aren't good with math, that is a significant ministry tenure of thirty-two years!) Bishop McMurray is remembered as a man with vision. When he came to Greater Bethany Apostolic Church, he changed the name to Greater Bethany Community Church. Bishop McMurray saw the need to expand the appeal of the church to those who were unfamiliar with the apostolic tradition. He had a vision of growing the ministry to include those who were unchurched. His vision succeeded: Greater Bethany Community Church had mass appeal throughout the greater Los Angeles area.

Bishop McMurray's vision for the future had him begin his ministry with its end in mind. Churches that do transitions well don't shy away from the fact that every pastor's tenure will eventually end. They confront this reality head-on by preparing for the transition before the day comes. They ensure that their pastors have good health care and retirement benefits; no pastor and or church should be held hostage because the pastor can't afford to retire. They also look ahead to the transition by studying the up-and-coming ministers who might be next in line. They discuss transition during the active tenure of the present pastor.

According to Deacon Joe Edwards, "Bishop McMurray was always a man who saw into the future. He started talking about his transition years before any of us saw it. He didn't wait until he was getting old or [had] taken ill." Bishop McMurray taught his deacon board and leadership team to think about the future. He knew that he, like every pastor, comes to leave. Bishop McMurray knew that his younger deacons would survive him, so he included them in leadership and prepared them and the church for transition.

The point has to be made that although the conversations Bishop McMurray had with his deacons appear insignificant, they speak to a larger reality: that Bishop McMurray recognized the need to protect his legacy in a well-planned transition. Taking a small church to a membership of more than 1,500 people had been significant. During Bishop McMurray's final years, with his failing health, attendance would suffer, however. For the church to resume its upward trajectory, a smooth transition was essential. Understanding this, Bishop McMurray was proactive. He exposed his church to some of the best talent in the ministry so they would know what to look for in their next pastor. He helped the leaders see clearly where he was pointing. Bishop McMurray saw his ministry extending into the life of his successor.

Joe Edwards has served as the chair of the deacon board since 1972. Deacon Edwards said, "Bishop McMurray talked to us long before he got ill. He let us know that it was ultimately our decision who the next pastor would be, but he wanted us to consider three people." The three preachers that Bishop McMurray wanted them to consider were young men whom Bishop McMurray had mentored over the years. One was his immediate assistant, and the other two were regular guest preachers who had a relationship with the church. The church knew these ministers, and each minister knew the church. When the time came for the church to make a decision about transition, it would not be starting from ground zero. Bishop McMurray had studied the congregation's interactions with the people, and I am sure he had a hunch about who would succeed him. Bishop McMurray's intentional act of bringing his potential successors into the life of the congregation was strategic. He didn't force his successor on the people, and he didn't choose for them. He observed and allowed these men to interact with the people. The people were given permission by their current pastor to have a quasi-pastoral relationship with their future pastor. Especially in a family-culture congregation, the outgoing pastor must give the congregation permission to love the next pastor. The senior must make way for the junior. Bishop McMurray did this by encouraging his congregation to dream about their future while he was present. They were taught that to think of the future wasn't a betrayal of the present.

In the end, the successor to Bishop McMurray would be Bishop Noel Jones. Bishop Jones wasn't a stranger to Greater Bethany Community Church; he had been doing a revival every January since the mid-1970s. Bishop Jones spent more and more time with Bishop McMurray over the years, as the two men became very close friends and developed a mentor-mentee relationship. Bishop McMurray was like a father in the ministry to Bishop Jones, and Bishop Jones emulated this giant in the tradition.

In 1992, Bishop McMurray's health began to take a turn for the worse. As the year progressed, Bishop Noel Jones was called in from Longview, Texas, to help out with the teaching and preaching. During those final years, Bishop Jones went from being the winter revival preacher to flying out each week to teach the Wednesday Bible class and to preach the Sunday-evening worship service. During Bishop McMurray's final year, Bishop Jones relocated to Los Angeles and lived across the street from the church, not only preaching and teaching, but assisting in all pastoral duties.

The wisdom of Bishop McMurray was that he had involved the deacon board so that, as these young preachers were coming through, the deacons knew what was going on. They were able to study the situation and observe how the potential successors related to the congregation, the present pastor, and the community. Consequently, the deacons were poised and prepared to make a decision about the next leader in a timely fashion. They had had years to study the situation, be in relationship with the potential successor, and understand the wisdom of the pastor whom they had grown to love while he shepherded that congregation for thirty-two years. Greater Bethany Community Church was a family church that was rich in the tradition of the Pentecostal Assemblies of the World. The transfer of leadership from Bishop McMurray to the next pastor had to be in the family, and it had to be someone who respected the father who had led the church for so long.

Bishop Jones and Bishop McMurray shared the key variable that had made Greater Bethany Community Church a great church: a love for preaching and teaching God's Word with excellence. When Bishop McMurray started bringing Bishop Jones out to teach and preach more regularly during his last year, he wasn't showing favoritism, and he wasn't picking the successor. According to Deacon Edwards, "Bishop McMurray wanted to make sure that the Word of God was being preached and taught with excellence. He cared enough about the people to make sure they got the Word. This is where Bishop Jones and Bishop McMurray were alike; they were both powerful preachers." Greater Bethany's leadership understood that the successor to Bishop McMurray had to be a great preacher. The church was centered on great preaching and powerful worship. The successor had to be a part of and had to honor that tradition.

The Sunday after Bishop McMurray's passing, the deacon board under the leadership of Deacon Joe Edwards put forth the name of Bishop Noel Jones to become the next pastor. Deacon Edwards said, "We didn't need to wait. We were prepared. We had seen how Bishop Jones loved the people and [how] the people loved him. We didn't even have to put the names of the other two gentlemen to the people. It was unanimous for Bishop Jones. Man, it was something." The church was ready for the transition. Bishop Jones had lived with the people and had walked with them through the death of their former pastor. Bishop Jones knew, loved, and respected his predecessor. The people saw that love and respect, and that knowledge enhanced his relationship with the congregation.

When a new pastor arrives, he or she has to understand that the people had a relationship with their former pastor, and in most cases loved and respected that pastor, especially if that pastor had been with them for many years. New pastors begin their own loving relationship with the people by letting them know that they also respect the former pastor and those who labored with that pastor.

Bishop Jones was clear when he said, "He [Bishop McMurray] respected my capacity and my ability, so he didn't hold back anything or any information I would need to be successful . . . We spent hours and hours talking about the church. He wanted to give it to someone who would carry on his legacy." Bishop McMurray saw the writing on the wall; he knew his days were numbered. He also knew that, though he hadn't forced him on the people, Bishop Jones was the chosen one. When Bishop Jones was called to be the pastor, the church didn't miss a beat. Bishop Jones said, "He [Bishop McMurray] didn't feel threatened. He was at a stage of life when he knew he wouldn't be around long. He knew I would take care of his family, and he knew I would do the right thing by him. That made it a lot easier."

Bishop Jones's role in the transition wasn't a passive holding on until his day came. He cared for Bishop McMurray and his family. By making the outgoing pastor and his or her family comfortable with the transition, the incoming pastor fuels the trajectory of the transition process. The family and supporters didn't have to engage in a battle with Bishop Jones because they, like Bishop McMurray, knew he would do the right thing by them. This is the trust factor. When a leader has the skills to lead, understands the areas of the church tradition that need to be maintained and enhanced, and is also trusted by the people, the sky is the limit.

Bishop Jones understood the legacy he inherited: "I understood that the whole Greater Bethany and the City of Refuge are his legacy. We enshrined his legacy; we named buildings after him, and we lifted his name up. I was intent to sustain and maintain his legacy." As Bishop Jones took the helm as the new pastor of Greater Bethany Community Church, he had analyzed the situation and understood that the preaching ministry was the foundation that needed to be expanded and enhanced. Bishop Jones put it this way, "I built upon the people's eagerness for the Word of God and the city's eagerness to have leadership that was transparent, genuine . . . [They] wanted theology that was psychologically inspired and wanted a leader who could articulate the Word on all levels."

Although Bishop Jones had inherited a rich tradition, he also entered a situation where the church was upside down. It had lost membership in the later years, after having a phenomenal ministry during the heyday of Bishop McMurray's tenure. When a pastor goes into a situation that is "upside down, there is not much to cling to. This type of transition is not difficult to proceed. It is almost like starting over. It's easy to prove your value as you turn the thing around," Bishop Jones explained. "Many of the people had left the church or stopped going to church all together. [In contrast,] when you go into a situation that is stable, it is difficult to prove your worth. People feel like you were handed something." Bishop Jones was left with a turnaround, and he built on it, expanded and improved with excellence, and the transition was successful. But even in a turnaround, a new pastor must make wise decisions, and those decisions must produce fruit.

If a leader in a turnaround makes decisions that don't produce fruit, people will begin to question his or her leadership, and this can hamper the trajectory of the transition.

Steps in the Growth Process

Step 1. Grow in Areas of Strength and Familiarity

Because of Bishop McMurray's proactive role in sharing the pastoral ministry at Greater Bethany before his passing, Bishop Jones arrived with a solid understanding already in place of who the church members were and what they needed as a congregation. When I asked Bishop Jones to identify the key to the growth of the church from hundreds of congregants when he first arrived to thousands within the first year. "Preaching with excellence that couldn't be denied or challenged" was his answer.

To take the church to the next level, he didn't violate the tradition of great preaching; he expanded it by identifying the needs of a changing community. Bishop Jones, unlike Bishop McMurray, was a theologian who used his theological proclivity to deal with the psychological aspect of the believer's life as a starting point in preaching. Bishop Jones's calling card was his psychological preaching, proclaimed by a leader who was genuine and transparent, who could preach to both PhDs and GEDs. This approach expanded the ministry by reaching more effectively into the diverse community that comprises Los Angeles. Within weeks of Bishop Jones taking over, the church membership ballooned.

When Bishop Jones became the pastor, the morning worship service was half full on a good Sunday; within months the morning worship service was overflowing. The church began to offer three morning worship services and one evening worship service on Sunday, and all of the services were packed. They were soon putting down chairs in the aisle and in the lobby; people would peek through the doors just to get a glimpse of worship. There were lines as people waited outside to be seated for the next worship service. The Wednesday Bible study was broadcast on a local radio station, and within months there were one thousand people attending the Bible study. Such rapid and substantial growth inevitably put stress on the original church members.

Step 2. Expand the Leadership to Suit the Ministry

Even though the people of Greater Bethany had voted unanimously for Bishop Jones to be their pastor, they had been voting for him to pastor them as they were at the time of Bishop McMurray's death: a church of a few hundred active members. When Bishop Jones took the helm and the church immediately started to grow, congregational care, pastoral leadership, and management had to be changed to minister to such a large congregation. There was obvious tension in the growth process. Those who had voted him in were taken aback by the transformation of the church from a family traditional church to an overnight megachurch.

How did Bishop Jones deal with his detractors and critics? He didn't fight them; he didn't call them out; he didn't put them off boards. He didn't incite a power struggle. He continued to preach with excellence, elevating the preaching ministry of the church, a tradition they valued, and he used it for the benefit of God, the city, the church, and the transition process. Even those who may have disagreed with the direction of the church and its growth couldn't argue with the excellence in biblical teaching that they experienced on Sunday and Wednesday. Greater Bethany also had a great music tradition. Bishop Jones didn't see this tradition in competition with the preaching ministry. He focused on retooling the music ministry by expanding its reach and competence. The lesson is that there is less resistance to the change process when the thing that fuels the change process is a part of the honored tradition of the church.

The growing congregation required additional leaders, so Bishop upgraded present leadership to the same level of the new leaders and partnered them together. He didn't remove people from leadership positions; instead, he tried to develop them at all costs so that they could remain a part of the team. He said, "I organized boards instead of individuals to run departments. I decentralized and expanded leadership."

Changes in leadership may also involve a transition in leadership styles—in the pulpit, in committee meetings, and in other aspects of church life. Bishop Jones recognized this as well. His predecessor had been a hands-on manager, but that wasn't Bishop Jones's style. What's more, the growth of church demanded change in the management style. To facilitate this transition, Bishop Jones spent time teaching his leaders, reorganizing the church while making the present leaders feel comfortable and secure in the transition.

Step 3: Help the Church Balance Past and Future

When a congregation grows quickly, as Greater Bethany did, church members of the past will find themselves overwhelmingly outnumbered by new members. They may discover that they have no choice but to move forward—and that sense of compulsion often inspires trepidation, resentment, and even hostility. The pastor and the lay leadership who find themselves facing such a situation still have to minister to all segments of the congregation while not holding the congregation back. The move forward must hold a healthy balance between acting in the now and ministering to the pain of those who are living in the past, even as they lead the congregation to its future.

Bishop Jones was intentional about this process. He said, "I had to integrate three broad constituencies. I had the crowd who had stayed through it all and felt entitled. I had the crowd who were returning and felt they still had a seat, and then I had the new people." A pastor who walks into a church that has these types of segments has to take integration seriously, or hostile camps will form within the church that will produce pain and chaos.

To Bishop Jones's advantage, he went into a situation that he could handle. As he had already been around the church for a full year, he knew some of what to expect and many of the obstacles to avoid. But regarding major changes, he said, "Before you begin to make any moves, you analyze and study the situation. You have to know where you are and how to handle the situation." A new pastor should not make a move if he or she hasn't considered the possible ripple effects. And every decision in the church is going to have major ripple effects, especially in a family culture congregation because the church is so intimately connected. If a pastor can't count the ripples, that pastor doesn't have enough information to make the decision.

Second, Bishop Jones said that any new pastors have to "try to find where the pocket of powers are and find out who you have to have in your corner in order to make the right moves." When it comes to making changes, pastors must know who has influence in the congregation, and these influencers must be supporters of the change and work within the congregation to affirm the direction God is leading the church under the new pastor.

Finally, in any transition, Bishop Jones advised other pastors to "reach for as many new people as you can because your power and your strength is not in the people who where there when you got there, but rather it is in the people who will come." The new pastor might be wise to build on existing ministry foundations, but Bishop Jones was also clear that a church has to embrace newcomers who have captured the new pastor's vision for growth and change. It is important to reach out to these new people, develop them, and integrate them into the life and leadership of the congregation. Bishop Jones clarified that a new pastor is not setting up a battle of old versus new, but is expanding the team. An incoming pastor is not trying to start a war in the church based on allegiance to the pastor. Rather, the new pastor is trying to lead the church into its future. In the case of Greater Bethany Community Church—which, under Bishop Noel Jones, would become The City of Refuge—the church would grow from a few hundred people to over 15,000 members.

The principles that informed Bishop Jones's transition— principles of open communication, honoring and building on the past, and cultivating new and existing leaders—have served him well since 1994. In his transition, Bishop Jones exemplified the wisdom of building on a church's existing tradition. At Greater Bethany Church, the core values of the church served him well. The value of great preaching and worship were vehicles that fueled the transition and moved the church forward. Bishop Jones helped Greater Bethany become even better at what they appreciated. A church that demands great preaching will not tolerate a mediocre sermonist, and Bishop Jones was a part of the great preaching tradition in the apostolic church. He was also a son of the church, who had a preaching style and flair similar to his predecessor, Bishop McMurray. Bishop Jones and Bishop McMurray also shared a common ethos of substantive preaching and teaching that eased the transition. In any transition, both the congregation and potential new pastor need to make sure that they share core values. When common values are shared, it is these values that become the glue of agreement in the moments of tension in transitions.

|6|

Following a Legend

Rev. Otis Moss III and
Trinity United Church of Christ

When one thinks about Trinity United Church of Christ (UCC) in Chicago, Illinois, it may seem like they have had only one pastor. Over my lifetime, Jeremiah Wright Jr. has become synonymous with Trinity, and for many of the members who worship there today, he is the only pastor they have known for most of their lives. He became an institution as he led his church and the nation in an Afrocentric movement that took the African American church back to its roots.

Iconic Church, Legendary Leader

Rev. Wright became Trinity's pastor in March 1972. He followed Rev. Dr. Kenneth B. Smith, the founding pastor, who led the church from 1961 to 1966. The church moved to a new site in 1966, and in 1967 the second pastor, Rev. Willie B. Jameson, took the helm. Rev. Dr. Reuben Sheares served as the interim pastor in 1971, and it was Dr. Shears who coined the phrase that would shape the call of the next pastor and the future direction of the church: "unashamedly Black and unapologetically Christian." With that mantra leading the thinking of the church, a young Rev. Jeremiah A. Wright Jr. became the pastor of Trinity at the age of thirty-one.

In 1986, they broke ground for their new worship center and began worshiping there in 1994. Dr. Wright led Trinity from a small family congregation of upper middle class blacks to a mass congregation that included the social elite and the brothers and sisters from around the corner. From 1972 to 2006, the church undertook an odyssey of growth as Dr. Wright led them to live their mantra of being unashamedly Black and unapologetically Christian. Over the next thirty-four years, a church of a few hundred grew to claim over 8,500 members.

I learned about Trinity Church in 1987 when I was a seminary student. I watched the PBS program *Frontline* that profiled Trinity as a part of its show "Keeping the Faith" with correspondent Roger Wilkins.[1] Like many of the seminarians on my campus and elsewhere during that time, I was inspired by Dr. Wright's embrace of Afrocentrism. This documentary, along with Dr. Wright's thriving ministry, put him and Trinity on the national scene.

Planning for Change

In 2005, after more than thirty years of ministry together, it was time for a change at Trinity UCC. As Dr. Wright began to contemplate retirement, he wanted to do all he could to make sure that the ministry continued to thrive. Dr. Wright and the congregation understood that they had to move on to the next pastor. Churches that do change well make transition a part of their ministry profile. The pastor and the members recognize when it is time to move on to the next phase in ministry. Dr. Wright became an active and willing agent in the church's change process. He made the deliberate decision to be participant in the transition in leadership at Trinity, caring enough about the church to do as much as he could to make sure the transition was a healthy one.

One key to a healthy, successful transition is the outgoing pastor's care for the future of the ministry. The predecessor has to have a vested interest in the success of his or her successor. This is especially true when the incoming pastor is following an icon or a legend; Dr. Wright was both. In the transition process, he understood his role and was mature enough to see how he could benefit his successor. But more importantly, he saw how he could assist the larger church and community.

Choosing a Successor

Rev. Otis Moss III was preaching a youth revival at Trinity. A young pastor of the hip-hop generation but also the son of a legendary civil rights–era pastoral legend himself, Rev. Moss was creative, energetic, and powerful in his preaching ministry. Not only did he have a deep appreciation for his cultural past, but he understood the cultural identity and idiom of the new generation and how to connect his Christian faith with the hip-hop generation. Seeing tremendous potential in the younger man, Dr. Wright approached Rev. Moss and asked him to consider being a candidate to succeed him at Trinity. Rev. Moss asked for time to consider the offer prayerfully and in discussion with his family.

Rev. Moss, along with his wife and immediate family, spent a year and a half in prayer and fasting, asking God what he would have them do as they looked at the next phase of Rev. Moss's ministry. When ministers make transitions from one church to the next, that change can't be about the church calling them or a career move, it has to be a move led by God. Rev. Moss recounted hearing Rev. Maurice Watson preaching at the Hampton University Ministers' Conference, as Rev. Watson reflected on his move from Omaha, Nebraska, to Macon, Georgia. He said, "Opportunity comes, opportunity goes, opportunity comes no more. . . . It is better to be in the downtown will of God rather than commute from the suburbs." It was at this moment that Rev. Moss knew he was to answer the call to Chicago. This sense of knowing is critical when moves are made; clergy and congregations must spend time in prayer and other spiritual disciplines as they seek to hear from God as they make moves to leave, call, and go.

In June 2006, Rev. Moss and his young family made their transition from Tabernacle Baptist Church in Augusta, Georgia, to Trinity United Church of Christ in Chicago. Rev. Moss didn't come in as copastor or senior pastor, but he came in as *the* pastor. This was an important designation because he didn't come in as pastor-in-waiting. As Rev. Moss came in as pastor, Dr. Wright walked with him over the next few months and steadily handed off pastoral duties. Dr. Wright was committed to retiring and turning over the reins.

Establishing a Covenant for Transition

Transitions that involve a retiring pastor need to clearly define when the retiring pastor is going to retire and how the transition of power is going to be handled. This has to be written, and all parties must be held accountable to the agreement. When icons or legends are alive and stay in the area, a smooth transition is even more difficult. In the minds of many church members, the iconic pastor is the only pastor they have had and the only pastor they want to have. Therefore, the lines of demarcation and transition must be defined to the minutest detail because the congregation is tied to the former pastor more in this context than in any other.

Transitions require intense discipline and hard work, but they can be made easier with preparation and managed follow-through. One powerful strategy for these transitions is the development of a covenant to be honored by all parties. The role of the former pastor needs to be clearly defined, in writing, especially when that pastor remains in the city or the congregation. May that pastor preach in that city? May he or she lead another church within one hundred miles of his or her former church? What are the written rules? This cannot be done unofficially; it must be in writing, signed, and legally binding. As the transition goes on, emotions and attitudes can change. The agreement needs to have teeth, with consequences if it is violated.

Pastor Moss had seen this kind of transition work effectively for his own father, Rev Otis Moss II, who had recently retired from Olivet Institutional Baptist Church in Cleveland, Ohio. Pastor Moss said of his dad, "He is clear he is just a member. He is a member with the title of pastor emeritus."

If the new marriage between new pastor and congregation is going to work, the predecessor and successor have to honor the same rule: one doesn't criticize the other. The covenant ensures that both pastors respect and support one another. The covenant should stipulate clearly that the former pastor doesn't take calls or complaints from church members or community leaders. The former pastor lets the church move on by removing him or herself from conversation about the direction of the church. This means that the former pastor must continue to remind his or her former members that he or she is no longer their pastor. This takes extraordinary discipline on the part of the former pastor. An intimate relationship has been formed between pastor and congregation, and now it must be radically redefined. In the case of Dr. Wright and Pastor Moss, they have kept their covenant, although Dr. Wright still maintains a relationship with his former congregation. Dr. Wright doesn't get involved in church issues; he doesn't take calls from staff about what is going on in the church. At Trinity, the mandate is clear: if a staff member calls the former pastor about a church issue, that act may be grounds for disciplinary action. These lines may seem harsh, but they are necessary if the transition is to be a successful one.

Establish a Transition Team

Another strategy recommended by Pastor Moss is the establishment of a transition team—a group of people who are committed to God and their church and who are fully vested in a successful transition. They don't have to agree with all that the new pastor says or does, but as Rev. Moss put it, "They have to believe that the new pastor is the one God has sent to lead this church and that his or her vision has the promise of bearing much fruit."

The transition team should be representative of the entire congregation. The team doesn't have to be large, but the membership should include representation of all the major constituencies in the church. Especially in larger congregations with complex relationships, there is no way a new pastor can understand the network of relationships in just a few years. The new pastor needs a team of trusted and committed leaders—individuals who can help guide the process of a healthy transition. This team's purpose is to advise the new pastor concerning roadblocks and congregational norms and to share with the pastor possible ways to think about negotiating and managing the change process.

In large congregations, good advice from Pastor Moss is that an outside consultant be employed to guide the process and deal with any problems that arise. I strongly agree with his suggestion. There needs to be an objective third party to deal with the issues that are a part of every transition. The third party could be a paid consultant, a firm, or a church consultant, who can also teach on the process of transition—but *not* a member of the church. This third party will make recommendations to the church as they navigate the transition process. The behind-the-scenes issues that surround a transition can throw a church into panic. Members won't understand what is happening, and therefore they won't know how to respond. They won't know if they should be alarmed. The congregation needs to be clear about how the transition is going to take place, and they need to be well-versed on the issues that will arise in the transition and how to deal with those issues in a healthy manner.

Respect the Past,
Moving into the Future

When a new pastor follows a legend, an icon, or a long-term pastor, he or she is confronted with a church culture where, for some in the congregation, the outgoing pastor is the only pastor they know. When the church has had phenomenal growth like Trinity, the church becomes a tri-part congregation: there are those who were there when the pastor was first appointed; there are those who came as the church was experiencing its major growth period; and then there is a third group that came at the tail end of the outgoing pastor's tenure. They are not from the past, don't fit in the middle, and are trying now to find their way in the midst of this transition. In the case of Trinity, Pastor Moss and the transition team are working to integrate these three parts of the congregation and to build for the future.

When I asked Pastor Moss how he was preparing Trinity and its leaders for the future, he was very clear: "We are focusing on Christ, community, and culture." Pastor Moss had to refocus the church by leading them in conversations about vision and the future. The guiding principles are how to lift up Christ and how to serve the community. *Community* as defined by Pastor Moss is a ten-block radius around the church. Just as Jesus calls believers to be in the world but not of it, Trinity is to be a church *in* the community but not *of* the community. The third piece is about culture: How will all that they do at Trinity highlight and celebrate African American culture and live out being Unashamedly Black and Unapologetically Christian in a postmodern world.

As Pastor Moss began to refocus the church, one of the first things he did was to help the church refresh how they saw themselves. He began with the media ministry. He used the website as a means to help the church begin to see themselves in their new face, by lifting up the three-pronged approach of Christ, community, and culture. He was careful to build on a principle that he found in practice when he arrived: the village. Pastor Moss asked, "As we build the village, what does that look like?"

Trinity has long had a Bible-college approach to Bible teaching; classes are offered seven evenings and six mornings a week, with online and audio course offerings as well. While honoring the tradition that was in place, Pastor Moss had to find creative ways to have those moments where he could walk with Trinity as they began to take a new look at themselves. When a pastor follows an icon, the church is prone to have tension between how see themselves as they were and how they will look in the future. In helping the church respect the past while simultaneously looking to the future, Pastor Moss said, "We go 'black' for three days. We have no meetings, nothing. What we do is the pastor teaches for three days. I taught on vision so the congregation could know what I was talking about. I then preached on the vision; we lived the vision." This was an important step in the transition. Pastor Moss didn't come in and radically altar the village approach to teaching; he embraced what was while tweaking the system in such a way that the congregation could hear what was to come. He used the past to build the future.

Pastor Moss understood that language carries culture; language also transforms culture. The church had to develop a new lexicon as to what it meant to be Trinity in 2006 and beyond. They had to understand what it meant to lift up Christ, community, and culture, and what that would look like moving forward. A church can't move forward if the members can't see where they are going. It is critical for the *church* to celebrate and build on the legacy of the past, not throw it away. There has to be a driving vision for the church to see the future, but draw from the past. This is especially the case when the church is full when the new pastor arrives. There is no sense of urgency for change. The church is literally comfortable. The new pastor has to come in and make them, in a loving fashion, *uncomfortable* with certain aspects (e.g., perhaps the youth ministry and health ministries are strong, but the congregation's beliefs can be stronger). This will be a moment of tension, as the new vision will stretch the congregation to grow. There will be dissenters, and some will leave the congregation as a result of the change in direction. Others will leave simply because, in every transition, there will be some attrition. The new pastor should not be alarmed by the attrition but accept it as a part of the transition, continuing to build on the past and chart a course for the future.

Introducing More Substantial Change

There should be a systematic process that allows for transition in the life of the church. Pastor Moss suggested that there might be a process by which, every six months or so, one third of the church's leaders should be up for transition, and this should include the staff in the church. "A path should be cleared," he explained. How? By establishing in writing that at regular intervals, key staff and lay leaders shall step down from their positions, including elders, deacons, trustees, and board of directors. The new pastor should reserve the right to intervene and choose to retain somebody, but the new pastor should be freed to build his or her leadership team. This means that it must be clear prior to the new pastor's arrival that this is the way things will go; people will step off. It is unfair to expect the present pastor to lead with the same team that the former pastor led. Pastor Wright built this aspect into his transition to ensure the new pastor would be able to create his own team. Some leaders would stay and others would have to be transitioned. The congregation needs to be prepared for the transition of members and church leaders and encouraged to support the new pastoral leadership team in this process. Transition must be done in love and respect. People who have served cannot be thrown away.

In the transition the goal is not to wipe out the past. The goal is to extend and build on the past. Pastor Moss said, "I built on the tradition of preaching, worship, and the rich identity that Trinity is committed to the village." The past was not destroyed or insulted by the incoming pastor. When you follow an icon or legend, Pastor Moss said, "you lose the right to criticize your predecessor . . . Your role is to be the *griot* [storyteller]." Pastor Moss is suggesting by his com-ments that the role of the successor is to celebrate and truly appreciate what he or she found upon coming. He or she is building on the legacy put in place by the predecessor and those who worked so hard with him or her. The storied history of the church has to be honored and extended by the successor.

Coping with the Pain of Transition

Even with a written covenant and a committed team in place, intentional pastoral transition is slow and painful. Dr. Wright made the transition out in an intentional process, not throwing everything on Pastor Moss's plate on day one. Pastor Moss had the opportunity to come and watch Dr. Wright in action and to observe the inner workings of the ministry—a time period for the successor to learn about the new ministry context and to digest the insights and lessons learned. For this learning process to work, both men had to be humble, and the congregation had to be patient and respectful.

In some ways, this process was like having a funeral and wedding in the same church, on the same day, at the same time. As the group Maze would say, "The same things that bring us joy, bring us pain."[2] The congregation, the retiring pastor, and the new pastor were experiencing joy and pain. They were willing to endure the conflicting feelings of joy and pain for the growth and development of the church. They realized that what they were going through was bigger than they were.

The transition was phased in over the first year, but who could have predicted that Trinity would again be thrown into the national limelight? When Senator Barack Obama, a member of Trinity, made public in his book *The Audacity of Hope*[3] that Rev. Wright was his pastor and had inspired him, the ensuing firestorm enveloped Pastor Otis Moss III and the entire pastoral transition process. They would have to deal with the media at every turn, not to mention death threats and hate mail, and this of course complicated the transition. In the midst of it all they appointed a transition team that would guide and manage the process. Because the national media attention did not allow Dr. Wright to step out of the limelight nor permit Pastor Moss to focus on the local ministry, the transition and pastoral installation had to be extended. Not until March 2008 had Dr. Wright turned everything over to Pastor Moss.

We have already established the congregational benefits of professional help when you are dealing with large churches, and especially when a new pastor is following an icon or legend. The shadow of following an icon or legend can raise serious identity questions for the new pastor as well. For clarity's sake, the new pastor must know who he or she is and cannot get into being compared with the former pastor. This sounds simple, but I have found that the shadow of an icon can haunt the new pastor. According to Pastor Moss, "Spiritual and psychological support and assessment for the predecessor and successor should be done." Again, I agree with his recommendation. These assessments will help them know what they will face in the transition and what issues they bring to the table. I would go so far as to suggest that both of them be provided with counseling support throughout the transition, paid for by the church.

We sometimes forget that the pastors themselves are being affected by the transition in profound ways. The depth of the effects of the transition on them is something that even they can't fully comprehend. A professional pastoral counselor should be partnered with them for weekly visits for one to three years. It takes five to ten years for the work of a transition in a large, mega-ministry when the pastor is following an icon or legend. During that interval, the pain index can increase geometrically to an unbearable, almost deafening, level. The pastor needs an outlet. For the pastor's and the church's sake, they don't want this outlet to be his or her preaching or teaching. The pastor needs to be helped to see clearly so that he or she can preach the gospel.

Transitions are painful but rewarding. With the right help, the pastor and the church can come through them healthy, but it takes time and effort. A healthy transition isn't an accident; rather, it is a result of doing the necessary hard spiritual, emotional, relational, and psychological work. Trinity is moving forward by doing the hard work. They are making hard decisions and crying while celebrating their future. It isn't easy, but it is necessary. As Pastor Moss leads, he is becoming the pastor that Trinity knows.

NOTES

1. Roger Wilkins, "Keeping the Faith," *Frontline*, PBS, June 16, 1987.
2. Maze featuring Frankie Beverly, *Joy and Pain*, "Joy and Pain," ©1980, 2004 The Right Stuff.
3. Barack Obama, *The Audacity of Hope: Thoughts on Reclaiming the American Dream* (New York: Crown Publishing Group, 2006).

|7|

Is God Pleased?

Rev. Dr. Frank Thomas and
Mississippi Boulevard Christian Church

....

Transitions are difficult. The first three years are going to be hell, no matter who you are or what you do. Don't take it personal.

—Rev. Dr. Frank Thomas

....

When I interviewed Rev. Dr. Frank Thomas in the summer of 2009, ten years after he had accepted the pastoral charge at Mississippi Boulevard Christian Church (popularly known as "the Boulevard") in Memphis, Tennessee, the first question I asked him was, "How did you use the grace period new pastors get when arriving at a new church?" He quickly replied, "I didn't have a honeymoon period." In his case, he walked into a fire that he hadn't started and wasn't aware of until he arrived on his first Sunday. He was caught in a battle between the trustees and the church council. "When I walked up the aisle my first Sunday, they hit me in the face." While he was smiling and excited about where God had brought him and his family, there were those in the congregation who had already lined up against the change that was about to take place.

The band of warriors who were resisting the change in leadership the strongest had started the battle. Those who stood the tallest and talked the loudest in the transition at the Boulevard would take it to the press, the courts, and the people. Before the battle was over, Mississippi Boulevard Christian Church had racked up $700,000 in legal fees, families had been torn apart, and church members had been voted out. As the fight evolved, it wasn't simply about the pastor and who he was or wasn't. It became an attack on the officers and the ones who had extended Dr. Thomas the contract and had signed that contract. The group that led the attack sued, claiming that their property rights had been violated. The pastor had to go to therapy, and the congregation had to call in an outside reconciliation team to deal with the fallout.

It Helps to Know the History

Whenever a church changes leadership, that pastor and this new tenure are linked to the history of that church. The members must share that history with the new pastor, and the new pastor must have a healthy respect for that past while simultaneously looking toward building developing a new future. In 1999, when Dr. Thomas walked in, he was compelled to reach all the way back to 1921.

In January 1921, the Mississippi Boulevard Christian Church became the first African American congregation in the city of Memphis to belong to the brotherhood of Christian Churches (Disciples of Christ). The first pastor, Rev. Blair Hunt, served for fifty-two years before passing the mantle to Elder Lee Edward Koonce in 1973. Elder Koonce became what I call an unintentional interim minister, bridging the Grace and peace between a legend and a successful successor until the church called Rev. Alvin O. Jackson to the pastorate in 1979.

During Rev. Jackson's tenure, the church experienced a major fire in October 1979. The church rebounded from the fire, renovated the physical plant, and the church took off.

Crisis in the life of a congregation—be it something like a literal fire or a figurative firestorm—is almost necessary for that church to have closure on the past and move forward. The fire of 1979 was a crisis point that became a point of closure and a new beginning as the church rallied around their new pastor. Out of the fire came the establishment of a radio ministry and an expanded outreach to the community, and Rev. Jackson's preaching and leadership led the church to experience phenomenal growth.

In August 1984, the church had outgrown its Mississippi Boulevard location, so they moved from the inner city to the Whitehaven community, where the church continued to grow. The move gave the church a 1,700-seat sanctuary, which they needed. As the church continued to expand, strains on the facility led them to make yet another move in October 1992, this time back to the inner city. The Mississippi Boulevard Christian Academy was founded in 1991, and the school flourished at the church's new location. Together, Rev. Jackson and the lay leaders had established a megachurch in Memphis. Rev. Jackson led the Boulevard for eighteen years before he accepted the call to National City Christian Church in Washington, DC.

Dr. Thomas's tenure is linked to this history. Though an abbreviated story, it helps us understand and appreciate what every transition is about: linking the present and the future. Dr. Thomas didn't walk into a place and by coincidence find thousands of folk waiting on him. Serious work had been done, a foundation had been laid, and a legacy established. As Paul wrote in 1 Corinthians 3:10: "According to the grace of God given to me, like a skilled master builder I laid a foundation, and someone else is building on it. Each builder must choose with care how to build on it" (NRSV). Dr. Thomas and the church soon discovered just how carefully they would have to build, because the congregation did not realize how destructive fellow believers can be in the midst of transitions.

When Battle Lines Are Drawn

When Dr. Thomas entered his first trustees' meeting on Monday, November 7, 1999, he got his first clear glimpse of the problem that would fuel the tension during his transition. Prior to his call to Mississippi Boulevard, the trustees had been the primary leaders in the church, at the center of the decision-making process. Upon Dr. Thomas's call, the church council, which according to the church bylaws was to be the entity that led the church, intended take its constitutional place in the church decision-making process. It had been the church council that had appointed a search committee to find the next pastor. The search committee's candidate had been Rev. Dr. Frank Thomas; in contrast, the trustees' candidate had been Rev. Thomas Lewis Murray. Rev. Murray was the first staff minister hired by Dr. Thomas's predecessor, and Rev. Murray had served as the interim senior pastor for a period of eighteen months prior to Dr. Thomas's installation. When there is an inside candidate, the intensity and propensity for a split congregation is aggravated. The incoming pastor has to spend some time working to heal that pain and reunite the congregation.

During our interview in the summer of 2009, Dr. Thomas recounted that first meeting with the trustees. The trustees asked him straight up, "Do you believe the trustees should run the church, or should the church council run the church?" He replied, "In writing, it says the church council should run the church, so I believe the church council should run the church." The trustees replied, "We will not lift one finger to help you; it's on." The battle lines had been drawn, and the central divisive issue had been identified.

Managing the Dark Side: Wedge Issues

Wedge issues—or what I refer to as the central divisive issues—are a part of the tension present in all transitions, whether they are real or perceived. Unfortunately, when issues are perceived, that perception becomes real, if in only the minds of those who choose to see them as such. These central divisive issues become the catalysts for the divisive process. Once the battle lines have been drawn and the central divisive issues have been identified, a process is birthed that will escalate, expand, and try to take over the life of a congregation.

What a new pastor must realize is that, as much as this situation appears to take away from ministry, he or she must be intentional in a ministry of confrontation, healing, peacemaking, and reconciliation. The new pastor must minister to the pain that is a part of the transition process. If the new pastor treats the wedge issues and the divisive process like a distraction, the results can be disastrous. The church will not move forward, and the transition may fail. The pastor has to be available, present, and actively involved in all segments of congregational life. The pain of transitions must be named. The people need to be told what is happening and helped to understand that conflict and pain in transition aren't weird or unusual. They need to be guided through these times as the pastor and the leadership team first allow them to talk about what is going on, and then the pastor teaches and preaches them through the transition process.

Becoming Pastor in Truth, Not Title

Transitions are caught in a time continuum between the past, present, and the future. What is happening in the midst of a transition can't be seen as an isolated set of incidents. It is about old fights, the present crisis, and the future direction. A part of Dr. Thomas's struggle was that he was following both a legend and an interim pastor, who was also a candidate for the pastor's position. He had come in and not only dethroned the trustees by following the church bylaws, but he had also won the pastorate over the opposition's candidate. As Dr. Thomas put it, "The success of your ministry has a lot to do with who you follow." A new pastor has to be conscious of how he or she handles the relationship of his or her predecessor's supporters.

A new pastor can't get in between that love the members have for their former pastor. In reality, although the new pastor is now installed, he or she has yet to become the pastor. As Rev. Dr. Johnie Carlisle, retired pastor of First African Methodist Episcopal Church in Pasadena California said, "People have to give you permission to pastor them." A title, appointment, or vote of the congregation does not make one a pastor. The pastoral relationship is won over time. In Dr. Thomas's case, this tension of loyalty and relationship was even more complicated as he had to deal with the trustees' pain and with the fact that the interim pastor really wasn't an interim pastor at all, but a candidate. None of the work of closure of the past and preparation for the new leadership had been done. He also had to deal with the legacy effect going on because he followed a legend in the person of Rev. Dr. Alvin O'Neal Jackson.

It is a church's responsibility to resolve issues and heal open wounds as much as possible, prior to bringing in a new pastor. Churches can't be in denial about the issues they have. At a minimum, a church must let the candidate know what he or she may be walking into. It does the church no good if a pastor walks in blind. Every church has its battles; they are a part of the life of the church.

Every pastor has to realize that before he or she walks into that pulpit to preach his or her first sermon there are those in the congregation who have decided that they don't want the change. There is also a group that is in support of the change, and there are people in the middle. While dealing with the pain of transitions, leadership must make sure they don't give too much attention to that group that is the most visible in fighting the change the congregation is going through. Not every transition will be as traumatic, as prolonged, or as ugly as the one at Mississippi Boulevard, but conflict in one form or another is nearly universal.

Learning from Others' Experience

In the end Dr. Thomas felt the need to share his story and write about his story. The lessons he learned are instructive for all churches and pastors who go through the process of transition. In an article that Dr. Thomas published in the Spring 2006 issue of *The African American Pulpit*, seven years into his transition, he identified six principles that served as guidelines for his journey:

1. Remember Jesus.
2. Stop taking it personally.
3. There are no victims, only volunteers.
4. Vindication takes time.
5. Do not fight battles with unspiritual weapons.
6. This is necessary.[1]

Let's review these six guidelines and expand them to speak not only from a pastor's perspective, but also from a congregational perspective. Transitions are not simply about the incoming pastor. As Dr. Thomas said when I interviewed him, the madness stopped when the people said *enough*. As churches go through transition and congregational conflict escalates, the seasoned and senior members of the church should be wise enough to stand and declare, "This is enough; it stops now."

Remember Jesus

The first principle that Dr. Thomas lifts up is, "Remember Jesus. He despised the shame, but endured."[2] Remember Jesus when the church is going through a transition and the tensions run high. In the case of Mississippi Boulevard, their transition became national news. Members had to face co-workers, family, and friends and deal with the embarrassment. When transitional struggles become public, members are forced to take positions defending the church and its leadership. They get tired of their church being dragged through the mud, their pastor being represented as the center of controversy. Many may decide to leave the church rather than continue to face the controversy.

We can look at this remembering Jesus in two ways. One, remember that this is Jesus' church, and we are serving him. Two, we have in Jesus a model of how to deal with humiliation. As Hebrews 12:2 suggests, Jesus despised the shame of the cross but he endured. The church has to be in transition for the long haul. In the transition we have to look to Jesus, who is the author and finisher of our faith, and who will finish the good work he has started. The pastor and the church have to be committed to seeing this transition through to the end.

Don't Take It Personally

When the church is going through transitional conflict, names are going to be called; people are going to make others the enemy. As Dr. Thomas says, "Stop taking it personally. It has nothing to do with you as a leader personally. You cannot keep this kind of stuff from happening. In some of these places, the church has to die to live again."[3]

I have worked with churches where they took the transitional tension personally and began to call names and attack each other's characters. When leadership responds personally or in the flesh, who will lead the healing and reconciliation process? Who will take God's way? Leaders in the church have to take what Dr. Thomas calls a systems view. They have be able to stand back and look at what is happening and act as leaders who want to move God's agenda forward.

No Victims, Only Volunteers

In the midst of transition Dr. Thomas reminds us, "There are no victims, only volunteers. . . by choosing to stay, I refused to become a victim of my circumstance; I volunteered for it.

God is pleased when we take personal responsibility and do not blame. Learn to declare: I am not a victim; I volunteered for this assignment."[4]

When I first read this, I applied it to the pastor who accepted the call or assignment, but upon further reflection I concluded this goes for all members of a congregation. In the life of the church, no one is held hostage. As a member, one can choose to leave and unite with another church. A church officer can choose to resign his or her position. A pastor can decide to leave and take a new charge somewhere else. We are volunteers in this drama. We have to take responsibility for the church relationship where we find ourselves. When we accept responsibility for these relationships, we are empowered as active social agents, and the Spirit of God empowers us to act. We can do something about our situation. Conversely, when we see ourselves as victims, we are being acted upon, and we react instead of acting. If we are going to be led by God in these moments of transition, we have to be actors instead of reactors.

Vindication Takes Time

The change process isn't overnight. It takes time. As Dr. Thomas said during our interview, "The first three years are going to be difficult no matter what. In year seven you get to the peak. In year ten, you get to do some things. It takes fifteen years to change a church. Ministries don't grow over night. It takes time." It is like running a marathon: I don't care how fast you are, it is going to take time to run 26.2 miles. In times of transition, leaders and congregations have to pace themselves. We can't hurry change. We can't hurry transformation. We can't hurry transition, healing, or reconciliation. The pain of the process will ultimately lead to God's being glorified.

"Vindication takes time. People can tear down in five minutes what it takes years to build. It is easy in this gossip-loving, like-to-see-people-fall culture for people to make accusations. They throw mud that takes years to clean off. I had to learn to wait and depend on God. God will vindicate, but it takes time and you just have to wait."[5] If God has called a new pastor, God will sustain and redeem that pastor and the church. This end is really the beginning. Before we move, we must make sure God is directing the steps.

Don't Fight with Unspiritual Weapons

It is important to keep an Ephesians 6:12 perspective: "our struggle is not against enemies of blood and flesh" (NRSV). This is the flip side of Dr. Thomas's earlier point: the conflict isn't personal. It isn't about taking sides against fellow church members. Transitional conflicts have two sides: God's side and the devil's side. Through prayer, fasting, and the pursuit of wise counsel, pastor and congregation alike may discern God's purpose and desire for the church. And then "God's side" may be empowered to engage the battle—keeping in mind that this is spiritual warfare. As 2 Corinthians 10:3-4 admonishes us: our weapons are not carnal. Indeed, the apostle Paul goes on to remind us that our most powerful weapons are instruments for building up, not tearing down. They are tools for nurturing mutual respect, deeper love, and increasing faith.

Conflict Is Necessary

As Dr. Thomas goes on to say, "This is necessary."[6] Yes, the pain and process of a transition are necessary. They force us to ask the essential questions, questions that get to issues of ecclesiology—who we are as a church. When I asked Dr. Thomas directly how he and the church got through this, he said, "We focused on our strengths. Whenever you are in a jam, you focus on your strengths. I focused on preaching; we focused on worship." In the midst of the transition he emphasized the importance of his devotionals life. As the church moves through the transition, it must be focused on being the church—on being the body of Christ at work in the world. As the church focuses on being the church, it will be the church of Jesus Christ and not the church of mess, gossip, backbiting, and infighting. The pain of the transition, which must be ministered to, can't become such a distraction that the church loses its focus.

When a church is focused in the midst of transition, they are empowered to get through the difficulties. They can see through the mess and actually see God. The church will have a sense of direction, even when their direction is being questioned and challenged. In the midst of a transition the challenge is to focus on going in the right direction. When a church is focused on being the body of Christ, they will receive a deeper sense of purpose and mission.

What Ministry Moves Cannot Miss

As I was ending my interview with Dr. Thomas, I asked him if there was anything I was missing. He replied, "Yeah, make sure that it is God calling you to a church. Moves in ministry can't be about the bigger church or seen as some career move." Ministry isn't about a career or climbing a ladder; ministry is about call. Ministers must be called to churches, and churches have to be clear who God is calling to lead them. What might look good and better may not be what God wants for this minister or this church. Ministers who take new churches can't be running from where they are. Churches shouldn't call a minister because they are in a rush to run from the last pastor. The process of pairing a congregation with pastoral leadership must be rooted in the call of God.

As Dr. Thomas ends his article, he says, "It took all of this for me to learn that you cannot please people. It took all of this for me to learn, 'If God is pleased'—that is all that really matters."[7] In times of difficult transitions this has to be the focus: Is God pleased? When we ask the question, "God, are you pleased with me and what I am doing in your name?" it gives us right perspective, the right motives, and leads right back to God. And it is God who called us in the beginning.

NOTES

1. Frank Thomas, "Is God Pleased?" *The African American Pulpit*, Spring 2006, 76.
2. Ibid.
3. Ibid.
4. Ibid.
5. Ibid.
6. Ibid.
7. Ibid.

|8|

Making History

Rev. Dr. Leslie D. Callahan and
St. Paul's Baptist Church

On May 31, 2009, at St. Paul's Baptist Church of Philadelphia, Pennsylvania, the new pastor, Rev. Dr. Leslie Callahan, would preach her inaugural sermon, "It's Time," from Acts 2:1-21. This was a major moment in the life of St. Paul's. Not only were they welcoming their new pastor, but they were welcoming the first female pastor in the historic church's 119-year history.

Ironically enough, the birth of this historic church was at the hands of two women. Mrs. Frances Fields and Mrs. Mary Henryhand led an effort in 1883 to establish a worshipping community in North Philadelphia. By 1889, thirteen others had joined them in this effort, and the group became known as the Morning Star Baptist Mission. In 1890, Rev. E. W. Johnson would become their pastor, and the mission became St. Paul's Baptist Church. More than a century later, the women who started the church can look down from heaven and see their legacy continue in the hands of their new daughter and pastor.

One of the present members responded to this historic day by saying, "I remember when women couldn't even stand in the pulpit to make announcements, and to see that day come when a woman would be the pastor of St. Paul's is just extraordinary." The pulpit in the African American community has long been a male-dominated space. This has especially been true in the African American Baptist tradition. What had emboldened St. Paul's to break with tradition and to call a woman to be their pastor? What unique issues do women face when they are called to lead a church that has historically been led by men?

A Clean, Professional Process

How does a church such as St. Paul's become open to calling a woman to be their pastor? Dr. Callahan is clear that one of the keys to her successful candidacy was that St. Paul's had a clean process. The search process was an open search rather than a selection committee, in that the committee didn't go into the search with a candidate preselected. Rather, they initiated the search, sincerely seeking that person whom God wanted for St. Paul's. The beginning of the pastor-congregation relationship begins in the search process, as candidates get a feel for the church. A search committee looks for candidates by opening the door, widely advertising the pastoral vacancy, and seeking the best candidate for the position. Candidates have to be treated with respect, as real people with hopes, dreams, and often families, people who are seeking the place where God is leading them.

Dr. Callahan was appreciative that at every turn the search committee kept the candidates up-to-date on both where the church was and where the candidates stood in the process. Dr. Callahan said, "The process was professional, and I felt like I was being taken seriously as a candidate." The committee asked for materials from the candidates as needed. Deadlines were set and honored, and the process had a linear progression.

The face of the search committee, the person who communicated with Dr. Callahan, was warm and welcoming. The person who is chosen to communicate with the candidates is representing the church. He or she has the significant responsibility and privilege of making the church's first impression on the candidates, so the church must choose someone who will reflect the values and the culture of the church.

A Fair and Critical Evaluation

Not only was the St. Paul's search process open and professional in its communications with the candidates, but the process was fair and critical in its evaluation of the applicants. Each candidate's credentials made a difference. In the case of Dr. Callahan, St. Paul's chose a preacher with impeccable character, postgraduate educational credentials, and compelling preaching skills.

Dr. Callahan's experience demands further comment. Her credentials speak to a truism in the African American church: Women still have to be more than qualified to even get a look from search committees. To look at Dr. Callahan's résumé is to be immediately impressed. She is not only well educated, but she is one of the most talented preachers in America. She has a Bachelor of Arts degree in religion from Harvard University, a Master of Divinity from Union Theological Seminary, and a Doctor of Philosophy from Princeton University. Men with credentials that can compare to Rev. Dr. Callahan's are hard to find. If she were a he, Dr. Callahan would have been competing to lead churches that have thousands of members.

When I asked Rev. Dr. Callahan about being "more than qualified," she was clear: she is happy and thankful to be at St. Paul's. In no way does she feel like it is a "lesser" church or that she somehow deserved more. This is the place where God has called her. She is overjoyed at having the privilege of serving St. Paul's and looks forward to a long tenure at the historic church.

Although sexism in the African American church is alive and well, the search committee gave her a look not simply because of her credentials but because they were open to God through prayer and seeking God's will as they extended a call to the next pastor.

Moving beyond Sexist Assumptions

So, how did St. Paul's deal with the issue of her being a woman? Dr. Callahan responds, "The church had done a lot of that work prior to me coming for my visit. I don't know exactly how they did it, but when I came for my visit, I didn't feel like I had to prove that I belonged at the table. I never got that what-are-we-doing-here feeling." The church had done the work of accepting and calling the best person to lead the congregation. The congregation had done the work of dealing with the fact that they might call a woman to be their pastor. There wasn't open resistance to Dr. Callahan when she arrived for her visit and after she was called. We have to assume that every member wasn't pleased with this historic move. But in the aftermath, we find that the church embraced their new pastor. The overwhelming majority of members has remained at St. Paul's and is supporting the move forward.

The keys to the church approach to the gender issue were centered in the openness of the search process. The process was so transparent throughout the life of the congregation that there wasn't room for backlash. There wasn't room to question if things were done decently and in order. The value of looking for the best person was central to the conversation within the congregation and among the search-committee members, and this value permeated all they did in the process.

We return to the process again and again. It has to be clean and transparent; the congregation must be brought along and included in the process as appropriate. When a call is to be issued and a vote has to be taken, the congregation must be educated and must be clear on the values that have informed the process. The values of openness, transparency, and seeking who God wants to lead the church—whether that person is male or female—have to be put on the table. Churches that are willing to have difficult conversations about sexism in the church and its negative ramifications will be the churches that will be open to calling the brightest and best to lead their churches. St. Paul's understood what skills and gifts they needed in their next pastor: a pastor who was a gifted preacher, with energy and leadership skills to grow the ministry.

From Proud History to Present Plateau

Although St. Paul's has a proud and strong history, by the end of the twentieth century, the church had hit a plateau. There was a need for renewed energy in leadership that would take the church into the future. From its birth under Rev. Edward William Johnson to a major expansion in the 1940s and 1950s under the leadership of Rev. Edwin Luther Cunningham, the church had grown its campus and outreach efforts. Rev. Cunningham was followed by Rev. Arthur Lee Johnson, who would lead the church for thirty-three years. While the church was vibrant and stable under the leadership of Rev. Arthur Johnson, this period was much different than what they had experienced during the tenures of Rev. Edward Johnson and Rev. Cunningham. After Rev. Arthur Johnson, Rev. C. Matthew Hudson would lead what is referred to as what is considered to be the "fourth era" of St. Paul's history.

The St. Paul's search process was guided by the need to find the pastor who could lead the church into the twenty-first century. The church understood where they were in time. The city and the nation were going through radical change, and the church understood that it needed a pastor who was traditional enough to honor their past and visionary enough to lead them into the future. In an age of brokenness and fragmentation in the African American community, the skills that women bring to the pulpit may be just what God has ordered. While churches shouldn't get locked in on gender, they shouldn't ignore it or allow it to be seen as a liability to be overcome. When a woman is a serious candidate, her gender should be seen as asset, not a liability.

Rev. Dr. Callahan recalls talking with one of the search-committee members after her selection. The church had received attention in the press—especially in the Philadelphia area—surrounding what was touted as an historical selection. The member told Dr. Callahan, "We had no idea we were doing something this big." As Dr. Callahan said, "The church wasn't trying to make a political statement. They weren't trying to break with tradition. They were bringing the best people they could bring, and there was a clear sign that the lot was falling upon me." St. Paul's wound up with a star. The key here is for the church and committee to be open to listening. As Dr. Callahan says, "You [the candidates] have to have something that stands out, but you have to have a committee that is willing to look. That is the game-changer." The committee has to be willing to hear a voice and look at a face that may not sound like or look like what they have historically recognized as a pastor. Dr. Callahan said, "The reality is that sexism is alive and well, and you got to deal with the fact you [as a woman] don't look like what a pastor is supposed to look like." The committee must listen not only to the preacher, but also to God. How is God using God's chosen vessel to speak to the congregation?

Embracing Women as Pastoral Leaders

One member remarked to Dr. Callahan, "I have never had a woman pastor before; we will see how this works out." For a lot of churches in the African American community, having a female pastor will be a new thing, but they have to be willing to try it out. They have to give it a chance to work. When I survey the best and brightest of the students with whom I have the privilege of sharing my life at Fuller Seminary, I am always struck by the fact that the best and brightest of our African American students are most often women. I celebrate this great gift God has given the church in the women who will lead our churches in the twenty-first century.

As a church makes the move to call a woman to be their pastor, one of the realities they are going to have to deal with is sexism. So how does a congregation confront sexism within the church? Dr. Callahan suggests that the pastor and congregational leaders must work together to let the congregation know that the church is in good hands. Dr. Callahan put it this way, "A sense that the church is in good hands puts the people at ease." While women have led our homes, communities, cities, and states, when we come to the church, folk often ask, "Can she do it?" The question, when reflected on logically, is ludicrous. Of course women can lead the church as the pastor; they are more than competent.

When we move beyond the competence question, some in the church may have been taught from an antiquated biblical interpretation that women shouldn't lead, despite clear examples such as Deborah and Miriam in the Old Testament and Priscilla and Phoebe in the New Testament. No matter what the root of the objection or question, when a pastor leads, takes care of the people, and—most importantly—preaches and teaches the Word of God, it is hard for anyone to raise questions. As Dr. Callahan says, "One of the challenges women have is getting to the point where someone will listen to a sermon. When you get your chance, you got to blow it away. You got to preach. You have to preach some way that people recognize it as preaching. You can't be timid." For years, people have looked in the pulpit and seen men. The pastor and the congregation in the midst of moving from male to female leadership can work intentionally to help people see women as pastors. This is a reimagining effort, and the church must embrace, support, and champion their new leader, and see her as a pastor in every sense of the word.

The Value of Key Supporters

The St. Paul's congregation has embraced Rev. Dr. Leslie Callahan in the role of pastor. Key support came from the elderly members in the church. The elders still have respect in the African American church, and when the elders support and embrace the pastor, that support makes a difference. Dr. Callahan shared a moment as she reflected about a ninety-seven-year-old member whom she eulogized. In the midst of the funeral, someone shared how proud the member had been for voting for Rev. Callahan. The sister was proud to have done something different. The senior members of St. Paul's remember the days of yore, and they know God has the power to do it again. They were central to supporting the move as Dr. Callahan came in and focused on worship and became a part of the legacy of St. Paul's. "You have to acknowledge the history. You have to respect where the church has been. I am trying to honor the history. I am honored to pastor a church that has had such great pastors. I try to honor and build on the history." says Dr. Callahan. The history of the church is that firm foundation. The history of the church is what the senior members hold dear. It can become a springboard for vision; as the senior members look back, they can see the future. They can see the twenty-first-century vision because they lived the twentieth-century vision. Don't fight the past, but embrace the past. Let the past testify to what God has done and what God will do again in a new way in this new era of the life of the church.

As many African American churches will find a rise in the number of female applicants who respond to the call to lead, how will they receive these résumés? To look for a man simply because he is a man is nothing but pure sexism and denies the voice of God as God speaks and directs a church to look at and listen to any and all qualified candidates—including women. A church that is bent on getting a man to lead may miss its blessing. St. Paul's focused on what they needed, and they invited God into the process to send them the right person. She was a blessing from God in the person of one of the brightest and most talented preachers in the nation. If the African American church is going to be that prophetic church God is calling it to be in the twenty-first century, the church must be willing to embrace a woman as pastor.

A Practical Postscript

Working Pages

Transition in pastoral leadership is one of the major—if not *the* major—decision a congregation or a denominational leader has to make in the life of a local church. It is a decision that can't be taken lightly and can't be done without a systematic approach that is led by the Holy Spirit. This portion of the book provides an outline for how a congregation or a denominational representative might think about processing the decision to call a new pastor. This process starts with prayer and seeking direction from God. The bishop or denominational leader, the congregation, and the prospective pastor all need to hear from God.

As much as God is in this process and leads this process, it is important to ask God the right questions. The tools in this chapter are prayer concerns. As you work through this process, it assumed that you are praying and reflecting on the data you amass in the project. We have to be open to the movement of the Spirit as we go into the search process for a church or a new pastor, but this doesn't mean the process will be without order, logic, and reasoning. It is important that we allow the process to minister to us. In many cases churches are stuck on the type of pastor they want, and there are so many pastors who are seeking a certain church that they don't allow the process to move them and lead them because the decision has been made before the process begins. Instead, I am suggesting that God is in the process, and the process works for the good if we allow the process to work. This means we enter the process keeping in mind that the end is what God wants and not what we want. In the process we want God to give us the desire for the pastor we need, or in the case of the pastor, the church we need.

Have We Said Our Goodbyes?

A part of the search process is the goodbye process. In the case of churches like the African Methodist Episcopal Church, the pastor and the congregation need to be mindful of the fact that they have annual appointments. Pastors and congregations should always be poised for transition. In many cases, a bishop will give a pastor a ninety-day letter, and when a pastor receives such a letter or has a hint about a possible move, he or she should make sure to prepare the church or at least the leadership for the transition. The first step in the transition process is saying goodbye.

Goodbyes Both Formal and Informal

The formal side of the goodbye can take the form of a dinner, a luncheon, or a portion of a worship experience. The church needs to publicly acknowledge that their pastor is leaving or may be leaving. This is a grieving process, and the church and the pastor must be allowed and even invited to grieve.

When a church is saying goodbye to a pastor, they must remember that this goodbye is just not for the pastor, but it also includes the pastor's family. Therefore, the goodbye event has to include the pastor and his or her family. This event is not just for the benefit of the pastor and his or her family, but is also for the benefit of the church family. Both the church and the pastor will benefit from this rite of passage, and the formal event itself should allow opportunities for the personal encounters that comprise the informal side of goodbyes—conversations, exchange of token gifts, hugs, and promises to remember one another in prayer.

Keys to Quality Goodbyes

1. There must be formal and informal ways for the church to say goodbye to their pastor and his or her family.
2. There must be formal and informal ways for a pastor and his or her family to say goodbye to their church.
3. The formal goodbye needs to be public and as inclusive as possible. It is important that members from every corner of congregational life can say goodbye to the pastor and his or her family.
4. The goodbye event should have a time where members can speak publicly about how they feel about the pastor and his or her family.
5. Official expressions of goodbye from ministries should not be allowed to mute other voices that want to share their love for the departing pastoral family.
6. The goodbye event needs to include pictures and video that celebrate the time the church has served with the pastoral family.
7. The invitation of other pastors and community personalities needs to be cleared through the pastor. Decide whether this a private family event or an open community event. Some churches may want to have two goodbye events. There could be a public goodbye that includes the larger community from outside the church, and then there might be an event for the congregation.

8. Pastors and their families need to say goodbye. They need to stand and express their feelings of gratitude to their church family. The pastor, his or her spouse, and children need to be allowed to speak and share as well. Pastors don't serve alone. Their families serve with them.

Cutting Ties with Love and Respect

When a pastor leaves a congregation, the relationship is severed but not ended. People in the congregation still love their pastor. They will miss their former pastor, and it may be years before the new pastor actually becomes "the pastor." As a congregation goes through transition, the former pastor and congregation have to decide how long the former pastor will be called to participate in major life transitions, such as funerals and weddings. While the relationship with the former pastor may have deep roots, at some point it becomes inappropriate for the former pastor to do funerals and weddings. The church needs to talk about this with the outgoing pastor and the incoming pastor. How will this be handled? How do they want to move forward?

When a pastor leaves a church, it is best for the pastors (new and former) to cut the ties from their former congregations. A pastor can't minister to two churches. The departing pastor shouldn't entertain conversations with former members about the new pastor and administration. That congregation will not be able to progress when the former pastor is constantly dipping into the church politics that are no longer under his or her oversight. Pastors, when you accept a new call, you have to let go of the old one. Congregations, the relationship with your new pastor will be hindered if you continue to run to your old pastor. The church and the pastor must move on. In the process of goodbyes, talk about how the church will move on and let go. Speak it aloud, wail, and weep, and God will move the church to the next stage.

Who Are We as a Church?
The Church Profile

As a church looks for a new pastor, and as pastors look for a new church, they need a process that gives the best chances for a quality search process that results in a good match. One of the worst things that can happen is a bad fit. A church must systematically decide who they are and what they need. The church needs to take time to reflect. When a denominational authority is appointing a pastor to a church, the congregation can present their findings from the congregational profile to the denominational leadership. The who are we question is answered initially by doing a congregational survey. The survey below can be administered during a worship service and can be collected via the offering basket.

A Congregational Survey

1. What is your age range?
   (a) under 15 (b) 16 to 20 (c) 21 to 39
   (d) 40 to 59 (e) 60 or above
2. What is your gender?
   (a) male (b) female
3. How would you describe your employment status?
   (a) student (b) caregiver / homemaker
   (c) blue collar worker (d) white collar worker
   (e) self-employed (f) unemployed
4. If employed in a profession, how would you describe your professional status?
   (a) laborer (b) educator (c) professional/executive
   (d) health-care provider (e) retail (f) other
5. Are you a member of this church?
   (a) Yes (b) No (c) Considering it
6. How many years have you been active in this church?
   (a) Less than a year (b) 1–3 years (c) 4–10 years
   (d) 11–15 years (3) more than 15 years

7. What is the distance between the church and your home?
    (a) less than 1 mile (b) 1–5 miles (c) 6–10 miles
    (d) 10–15 miles (e) more than 15 miles
8. How many of your family members are active in the church?
    (a) just me (b) 2 to 3 (c) 4 to 6 (d) 7 or more
9. Five years from now, would you want to see the congregation
    (a) stay at its current size (b) grow 10% larger
    (c) grow 50% larger (d) grow twice as large
10. What should our congregation be known for (choose two)?
    (a) preaching ministry (b) music ministry
    (c) outreach to the community (d) serving youth
    (e) serving young adults (f) serving adults
    (g) serving the elderly (h) worship
11. When you think about the church/campus (the physical plant), do you think
    (a) it is in good shape
    (b) it needs renovation/modernization
    (c) it needs major improvements
    (d) we need more space
    (e) we need to move or purchase new facilities
12. How often do you attend Bible study or Sunday school?
    (a) never (b) once to twice a month
    (c) three to four times per month (d) irregularly
13. What are the two most important issues in the life of the church (choose two)?
    (a) numbers/size of congregation
    (b) spiritual growth/discipleship
    (c) teaching/preaching of the Word (d) ministry
    (e) social action/outreach (f) evangelism (g) music
14. What is one thing you would want our new pastor to know about us?
15. What question(s) do you have for our potential new pastor?

A Screening Team,
Not a Search Committee

I deliberately call this team the *screening team* and not a search committee. The name designation is significant because it tells what the role of the team should be: a group of people who screen the potential pastoral candidates and then forward them to the larger congregation. They present the candidates, and then the congregation becomes involved in the process of selection. They aren't searching; they are screening. This team should represent all pockets of the congregation: long-time members, new members, emerging members, working class, middle class, upper class, male, female, youth, young adults, adults, and seniors. The breadth of the screening team ensures that all voices are heard throughout the process, not simply at the vote. The screening team should reflect upon the congregational survey and let it inform how they answer the following questions as they begin the screening process.

What Are We Looking for in a Pastor?

1. What type of pastor is our present pastor? What type of preacher is our present pastor? What type of preacher do we want our new pastor to be? (e.g., lecturer/teacher or whooper/preacher, traditional or nontraditional)
2. What kind of leader is our present pastor, and what type of leader do we need in the next pastor? (e.g., priestly, prophetic, nationalist, or political)
3. What style of management do we want in our pastoral leader? (e.g., hands-on or hands-off, detail-oriented or big-picture focused, visionary or administrative, fiscally conservative or risk-taker)
4. What is the age of our present pastor, and what is the age range we want our new pastor be in? (Also to be

considered is the age of our present pastor when he or she came to our church.)

5. What type of education did our present pastor have, and what type of training do we want our new pastor to have and why? (e.g., level of education, content of education, level of other life or vocational experience)

6. How much pastoral experience did our present pastor have when he or she came to our church, and how much experience do we want our new pastor to have? (e.g., number of years as senior pastor or as an associate-level minister)

7. What type of congregation are we in terms of size, and what type of congregation do we want our new pastor to have come from? (e.g., family-size [50–100 members], pastoral-size [101–350], program-size [351–999], corporate-size [1000–3000], mega-size [3001+])

8. What type of biblical teacher is our present pastor, and what type of teacher do we want our new pastor to be? (e.g., expository, topical, word-study, book of Bible) What are the weekly teaching expectations? (e.g., mid-week Bible study, Sunday school, teacher training)

9. What is the marital status of our present pastor, and what do we prefer for the marital status of our new pastor? (e.g., single-never married, divorced, widowed, newly married, long married, remarried)

10. What is the family status of our present pastor, and what do we want the family status to be of our new pastor? (e.g., infant/toddlers, school-aged, teenaged, young adult, empty nest)

11. What is the health and fitness standard of our present pastor and what do we want the health and fitness of our new pastor to be? Why? (e.g., issues of weight, general health, ability)

12. What is the gender of our present pastor and what is our preference for our new pastor?

The committee should work through these questions. Of course you will not publish your thoughts and answers to all of the questions, but in conversation, you should explore your working assumptions about what you are looking for in the new pastor—and why. If the consensus unearths some undesirable prejudices (based on race, gender, ability, age, or other factors), take the time to explore those issues. Some may need to be addressed with further education, biblical or otherwise. Some may need to be rooted out through exposure and prayer.

Having dealt with any ungodliness in your assumptions, you might share your answers to these questions with a bishop or other denominational leader who would be sending a pastor to your church. In many cases denominational leaders are not in touch with the churches under their jurisdiction, and they may have never asked what a specific local church wants in a pastor. And to be fair, on many occasions, churches haven't thought about what they want and what they need.

These questions demand critical reflection and should be answered very seriously and prayerfully. When looking for a new pastor nothing should be taken for granted. For pastors looking for a church, these questions should be in the forefront of your discussion with a church. Make sure you know what they are looking for, whether you fit what they are looking for, and what you are looking for. At the end of this process should come not only a profile of what the church is looking for in a new pastor, but there should also be a design for a position description.

The Position Description: What Is the New Pastor to Do?

The screening team should be empowered to work along with the personnel office (if the church has one) or denominational representatives in developing a position description for the new pastor. At a minimum the position description should cover the following:

1. Preaching duties and expectations: How many sermons per Sunday, per month? How many Sundays is it acceptable for the pastor to be out of the pulpit, preaching elsewhere?

2. Bible study: What is expected in terms of weekly Bible study teaching or Sunday school?

3. Preparation time: How much time per week is allotted for the pastor's preparation of Bible studies and sermons? (A pastor can't preach or teach effectively if time isn't scheduled for preparation.)

4. Family time: How much time is the pastor expected to spend with his or her family per week, and how will the church protect the pastor so that he or she has that time with family?

5. Leadership development: How much time is the pastor expected to spend teaching and developing leaders in the church?

6. Committee meetings and attendance: What meetings is the pastor expected to attend, from board meetings to ministry/committee meetings?

7. Visitation: What role will the pastor play in visiting members who are sick or elderly?

8. Funerals: Is the pastor expected to do all funerals, some funerals, or no funerals?

9. Weddings: What is the expectation of the pastor in terms of performing weddings and premarital counseling?

10. Counseling: What are the expectations on the pastor to counsel married couples, families in crisis, and individuals on other matters?

11. Office hours: How many hours per week is the pastor expected to be available on campus, in his or her office?

12. Travel and revival schedule: What is acceptable for the pastor as a revivalist or evangelist: how many days

per week, how many weeks per month, or how many months per year should the pastor be away preaching or teaching? How will the expenses of such travel (e.g., mileage, airfare, meals, etc.) be covered?

13. Sabbatical: How much time per year is the pastor expected to take to rest and renew himself or herself by spending time at professional conferences or in defined and designed study breaks?

Whom Will God Send to Lead This Congregation?

As the screening committee works through the work of who are we, where have we been, and where are we going, the dialogue stimulated from these exercises should inform the advertisement they write. When a church advertises that they are searching for a new pastor, they need to advertise as widely as possible while making sure their advertisement says who they are, what they hope to become, and what they need in a pastor who can appreciate their past while leading them into the future.

The screening committee must maintain the confidentiality of its proceedings and the files of the candidates. The screening committee will be handling personal information, and the information must be protected with the utmost of discreetness. Below is an outline of tasks the committee needs to accomplish as they begin their work.

Tracking Information about Candidates: Managing the Process

1. What is your timeline for the process from start to finish? You might want to break it down into segments of the process:
   a. From ad placement to new pastor in place
   b. Candidate interviews and observations
   c. Selection of final candidates for vote

    d. Offer to chosen candidate

    e. Official date of new pastor's start

2. Develop a plan for evaluating the candidates.

    a. Will they visit your church or will you go to their current ministry setting?

    b. If the candidates visit you, what will their schedule look like?

    c. Will they come for a week or a weekend?

    d. Will they preach a sample sermon or just teach a Bible study class?

    e. Will their families be included in the visit? If so, who will host them?

    f. What will the role of various church leaders be during the candidate's visit?

    g. What is the role of the congregation during the visit and in the selection process?

3. Draft job description and position advertisement.

4. Draft evaluation form for candidate files.

    a. Develop a checklist for files: résumé, academic transcript(s), ordination paper, letter(s) of reference

    b. Consult legal counsel before doing background check(s)[1], including credit history, public records search, criminal history, child abuse clearance.

    c. Request sample sermon(s) in manuscript or audio form as well as writing sample(s), whether published articles or routine congregational correspondence.

5. Design rating system for candidates, including an evaluation sheet (an objective tool that will help you rate candidates).

6. Place advertisement.

7. Design process to receive files, including who will receive the materials and who will establish and maintain each new candidate's folder.

8. Set regular meetings to review files as a committee.

9. Send response letters or emails to candidates, keeping all candidates informed on the process. You should be in contact with candidates at least every two weeks.

10. Publish publicly to the congregation the advertisement, the timeline for actions, and what the selection process is going to be. Everyone in the congregation needs to see the big picture and what his or her role will be in the seeking process.
11. Have a formal way for communication to flow from the screening team to the larger congregation. Design a way to openly and regularly communicate what is going on.

The Search/Call/Appointment Process and Contract Issues

When an invitation for leadership is extended to a potential new pastor that begins a process of negotiation. The word here is to be fair! A pastor needs to be reasonable in his or her requests, and a church needs to try as best they can to meet the needs of the new pastor. As the negotiations begin, the first order of business is not what the former pastor received, but rather, what does our present pastor need to be successful in supporting his or her family and serving our church? When negotiating a pastoral contract at minimum the following need to be covered.

The Move and Start-up Date

How will the move be paid for if the pastor and his or her family will be relocating? How much will be covered in the move? When is the official start date? When will benefits begin for the pastor and family? How long will the pastor have to settle into their new home, office and city? The first few weeks or months, the church has to be cognizant that the pastor and his or her family are trying to get settled. There will be a lot of demands on the new pastor. Their time needs to be protected so that the pastor and his or her family can get settled. The leadership board at the church needs to be on the front line by communicating the same to the congregation and working with the pastor to protect him or her.

Housing Allowance or Parsonage

Will the pastor be required to live in the parsonage if there is one, or is it the pastoral family's decision where they live and they will be duly provided a housing allowance? This needs to be negotiated up front. If there isn't a parsonage and the pastoral family will have to secure their own housing, will their purchase of new property be done through the church and become church property? Will the pastoral family stay in their present home or in a home they purchase and a housing allowance cover their expenses? With a housing allowance or parsonage, what bills will the church cover?

If the pastor stays in a parsonage, when and how will the property be inspected? What authority does the pastoral family have to make changes and upgrades to the home, and who pays for the upgrades? How is landscaping taken care of, who has the authority to change it, and who pays for it? (Generally speaking, the one who pays also is the one who assesses and approves changes.) Is the pastor expected to make the pastoral home available for church events? If the pastor uses the pastoral residence for church events, will support be provided for set-up and clean-up? Who pays for the events? If members of the pastoral family are disabled and structural accommodations need to be made to the pastoral residence, who pays? If a pastor lives in church-owned property, will he or she receive an annual or monthly equity allowance? Equity allowances are generally provided because a pastor who lives in church owned property cannot build equity.

FICA

How will employment taxes be handled? In the case of ministers, they are considered self-employed and have to pay their portion of taxes and the employer portion. Churches can supplement a pastor's income to help offset this burden and/or can deduct a predetermined amount from each paycheck that is put in an account for making the quarterly tax payments.

Pension, Health, and Other Insurance

What will be the church's contribution to the pastor's retirement/pension? Health and other insurance needs should be clearly established, and who will pay for what needs to be clearly delineated.

Professional Expenses

What are legitimate professional expenses that the pastor will incur and that the church will be responsible for? This list needs to be clearly articulated line by line: books, journals, conference attendance, memberships to professional organizations, travel to conferences, meals, travel to see parishioners, car allowance, clergy uniforms. If the spouse and pastoral family are traveling with the pastor on official business, are their meals and other expenses covered? Is there a limit on meals, travel, and other expenses? Is there an expectation that the pastor will travel coach, business class, or first class? What are the expectations for hotels: is it two stars, three stars, four stars, or five stars?

Sickness and Disability

How many days are allotted for pastor's illness? How will the church handle long-term disability or illness? Will the church pay for long-term disability? How will the church address the situation if the pastor is ill for a prolonged period of time (three months or more)? What is the procedure to fill the pulpit (short term and long term)?

Ministry Performance Conversations

In many African American churches there isn't a place to have a conversation with the pastor about his or her performance.

This has to be reconsidered. In the negotiation process the church and the pastor need to have a conversation and put in place a process for the congregation or a designated group to reflect with the pastor on his or her leadership. This conversation could take the form of a formal or informal review. In the case of reviews, there needs to be a plan as to how the parties will resolve issues arising from the review. How will the review team and the pastor be held accountable? If the review team is not pleased with the pastor's performance, how will that be handled? What are the consequences? What are the limits of the review body?

Process of Termination

There should be a clearly defined process and procedure for termination of a pastoral relationship. This goes both ways: if a pastor wants to leave the church and/or if the church wants to terminate the relationship. What will severance be in cases of termination? What constitutes reasons for termination? What happens to support for the pastoral family if a pastor dies? How long will they receive support from the church, including living in church-owned property?

New Pastor Orientation: Telling Our Story

When the new pastor arrives, all-important documents need to be at his or her disposal. Included among those documents should be copies of all policies and practices related to how the church handles business, such as church by-laws, constitution, or covenant, as well as more legal documentation of insurance.

There should also be a document, supported by pictures, reports, budgets, etc. that gives the new pastor a glimpse of the church. A document that charts the church's milestones should be outlined for

- the last five years;
- 6 to 10 years ago;
- 11 through 20 years ago.
- What will be the next chapter? Where do we think we are going? Let the pastor hear what vision the church has for themselves.

Of course, this postscript can only skim the surface of such practical matters. There are numerous other books written on the pragmatic details of pastoral transition, for both the incoming pastor and for the church and church leaders. Avail yourself of such resources, as well as the materials provided through your denomination and local judicatory. The more information you have at your disposal, the more prepared your African American congregation will be to accommodate the multitude of changes involved in any pastoral transition.

NOTE

1. Don't hedge on the background checks. If there isn't anything to hide, potential candidates shouldn't frown on the background check. Make sure the background check is done prior to inviting a candidate to your church and brought in front of the congregation. If things that need to be discussed come out of the background check, then invite the candidate to explain.

Afterword

One of the great blind spots for those persons entering seminary with aspirations of going into ministry is an inability to think about their departure. Frequently, persons are so eager preparing themselves to enter a place that they are unable to think about their exit. For that reason alone, I would suggest that *Leading Your African American Church through Pastoral Transition* by Rev. Dr. Ralph Watkins should be mandatory reading for anyone seeking to do professional church leadership.

This text is appropriate for anyone currently serving in a church. It is not just timely for those who are anticipating a transition; it is important for those who expect that transition is still a number of years away. Dr. Watkins gives helpful insights about how one should conduct one's time of service in a congregation even as one anticipates one's departure, however soon or far away. As the author quotes at one point, "We all come to go."

This practical resource will be especially helpful to those who anticipate transition within the next 5-10 years. The author shows how far ahead one needs to be thinking about the work of transition, and the value of cultivating a person who might be able to come in with a love of the people already in place, as in the case of Bishop Robert Wilson McMurray and Bishop Noel Jones. I particularly appreciated how the author studied situations where the transition went smoothly, identifying for the reader the core needs of those congregations and what gifts and skills the successors needed to possess.

Writing from a depth of experience, Dr. Watkins was willing to be transparent enough to talk about his own successes and failures as one who has had to endure the difficult seasons of transitions. His willingness to highlight his own learnings should help others who will inevitably face some of the same issues. The reader is the better because of it.

I am also grateful for the discussion about the needs of the pastoral family. Attention to these loved ones is critical because when the new pastor has a family, every member of that family is also making the transition. Dr. Watkins even includes a single pastoral parent in this discussion!

Also valuable is the book's discussion of transitions wherein the departure of the former minister happened as a result of conflict or involuntary separation. This reality is becoming disturbingly familiar, and ministers who seek to pastor people after such an event need to be particularly sensitive about unspoken wounds that might make the transition period even longer and more difficult. The author gives churches and ministers some tools and specific metrics they can apply to a process that must be undergirded by prayer and the seeking of the Holy Spirit.

Having just engaged a pastoral transition of my own, I am keenly aware of the need for this important work by Ralph C. Watkins. Even though I thought I had been preparing myself and the congregation I served for my departure, as I walked through my own transition I realized just how demanding this process is, even when anticipated. Pastors must allow themselves and their members to rejoice, grieve, celebrate, and prepare for as much as they can, and then allow themselves to live through the unexpected. *Leading Your African American Church through Pastoral Transition* will be invaluable to pastors and congregations alike, for all who are serious about the work of ministry we have been called to do.

Rev. Dr. Walter L. Parrish III
General Secretary
Progressive National Baptist Convention, Inc.